Anderson, Ken,
1952-

C 77

You can't do that,
Dan Moody!

34880030031277

$15.95

DATE			

You Can't Do That, Dan Moody!

The Klan Fighting Governor of Texas

by

Ken Anderson

EAKIN PRESS ★ Austin, Texas

Cover art by Mark Mitchell

Second Printing

Copyright © 1998
By Ken Anderson

Published in the United States of America
By Eakin Press
A Division of Sunbelt Media, Inc.
P.O. Drawer 90159
Austin, Texas 78709
email: eakinpub@sig.net

3 4 5 6 7 8 9

ISBN 1-57168-181-7

To my Grandparents
Carl and Jennie Anderson
George and Marion Harper

A formal portrait of Dan Moody, Texas' youngest governor. Photo courtesy of Austin History Center, Austin Public Library.

Contents

Ku Klux Klan rally near Lone Wolf, Oklahoma. Photo courtesy of Western History Collections, University of Oklahoma Libraries.

Acknowledgments

I especially need to thank two people for their help in making this book a reality. Clara Scarbrough wrote a very thorough, excellent history of Williamson County, which contains several pages about Dan Moody. Mary Jean Livingood, the director of the Moody Museum in Taylor, shared the museum contents with me and allowed me to view the house where Dan grew up.

I also need to thank Angela Dorau, the archivist of the State Bar of Texas, for sharing her research about the history of women and the law with me. The staffs at the Austin History Center, the Center for American History at The University of Texas, and the Texas State Archives were very helpful. Also, Bonnie Campbell, State Preservation Board, and Wayne Benedict, Williamson County maintenance supervisor, were very helpful in providing me with the floor plans of the capitol and the Williamson County Courthouse as they existed during the time Dan Moody worked there. Also, Judge Jim Bitz gave me access to his courtroom.

Finally, I'd like to mention my grandparents, to whom this book is dedicated. Three of them were born in Europe and immigrated through Ellis Island to seek a better life in America. My grandfathers worked hard in Pennsylvania coal mines and factories to make a better life for their families. They were "foreign born," one of the groups that the Klan directed its campaign of hate and terror against in the 1920s. But it was the values of my grandparents — hard work, honesty, perseverance, and faith — not the hatred championed by the Klan, that prevailed and made the United States the prosperous society it is today. My grandparents never had an opportunity to write a book, but I never forgot that my opportunities and value system came from them.

Taylor School. The school Dan Moody attended in Taylor. Notice the boys are barefooted. Photo courtesy Taylor Public Library, Archives Section.

1

"You're Too Young!"

"Daniel!"

"Daniel J. Moody! I know you can hear me. Come into the house now."

Oh, that voice. It was ten-year-old Daniel's lot in life to have a mother who was a former school teacher. She knew everything. Daniel soon hid his electric-generating gizmo where he could retrieve it before school the next morning.

"Yes, ma'am," Daniel said as he came running into the kitchen. Nancy Elizabeth Robertson Moody was an attractive woman who had a countenance that was perfect for child rearing. As a school teacher, Miss Nannie had been popular but strict.

"Daniel, your bedroom floor is a mess. There are wires and scraps of metal all over. You and your electricity! What ever happened to your dream of being a lawyer?"

"Well, ma'am, whenever I see Uncle John at the courthouse I want to be exactly like him. But my gizmos—"

"Well, never mind your gizmos. Clean up the floor and then get to your milking. You want to be done before your father gets home."

Daniel cleaned up his mess. Outside, he ran down the road a short distance to the dairy. Someday he would be old enough to drive the milk wagon, but for now, he would ride in the back and run up to customers' homes with their milk.

As Daniel milked the cows, he looked out of the barn across the field at the massive three-story school building. His school was one of the biggest, tallest buildings in Taylor, Texas. There it stood with its tall tower in the middle. Tomorrow would be Daniel's big day. He was going to sneak his latest invention to school to show all the other boys. But for now, Daniel had cows to milk and customers waiting.

"Dinner. Come to dinner," Daniel's mother called. Daniel and his twelve-year-old sister Mary came to the dining room table, where Daniel's father was already seated.

Even though he was a tall man, his huge, white beard—nearly a foot long—made him look even taller. "You can't believe how much Taylor has changed since I first came here," he said. "We would drive huge cattle herds, sometimes up to ten thousand head, all the way up the Chisholm Trail to Kansas. You can't imagine what the sound and smell of thousands of cows is like."

"*Pee-yu!*" Daniel held his nose.

"Don't be so yucky," scolded his sister.

"Children, no bickering," said their mother.

"I know what a dozen cows smell like from the dairy," said Daniel. "Thousands must have been awful."

"Well, the railroads changed everything," continued their father. "The Chisholm Trail is only a memory."

"Taylor wouldn't have started at all without the railroad," said Mrs. Moody.

"That's right," said Mr. Moody. "The Chisholm Trail ran twenty miles west of here, through Round Rock and Georgetown. When I came to Taylor for the I.G.&N., the rail lines had recently been laid, and there was nothing but farmland. Now, we are a full-fledged town, one of the most important cotton shipping centers in the country."

"It is an exciting time for you children to be growing up," said their mother.

"But even with all the exciting things going on, I want you two to know there is no quick trip to success. You need to keep up your education," said Mr. Moody. "It's hard work and honesty will get you ahead."

The next morning, Daniel got up at five A.M., finished with the cows and his milk route, and returned home.

"Mary, it's time for school," he called.

He didn't have to say it twice. Mary came running out of the house. The school was only two blocks away, but Daniel always stopped to get his older sister. This day, he also needed to retrieve his electric gizmo from where he had left it behind the bushes.

Gizmo in hand, he walked beside Mary. The schoolyard was huge and filled with children. The students didn't wear uniforms, but from a distance it looked like all the boys wore white cotton shirts and dark knickers and were barefooted and all the girls wore pastel cotton dresses.

The other kids were starting to file into class, so Daniel and Mary hurried. Once inside, they each went to their classrooms. Daniel was in fifth grade. Miss Gertrude Eckhardt was his teacher, but she wasn't there yet.

The boys gathered around Daniel's desk.

"It'll make electricity," explained Daniel. "All you have to do is turn this crank."

The kids buzzed with excitement.

"Oh, yeah?" said Billy Hayes. "It looks like nothing but a piece of junk to me."

Billy and Daniel had never been great friends.

3

But Daniel was surprised that Billy would challenge him on something concerning electricity. After all, Daniel knew electricity.

"Well, if you don't think it will work, put your hand right there," Daniel heard himself saying.

"Nothing but a piece of junk," repeated Billy as he took up the challenge.

Oh well, thought Daniel. *I'll have to prove my point.*

Billy's hand was in place. All the kids crowded around to see. Daniel hoped it really would work. He gave the crank a swift turn.

Billy's howl could be heard down the hall. Billy's reaction set the kids to running. One tripped and another fell over a desk. Then Miss Eckhardt walked through the door.

Silence descended on the classroom immediately. Miss Eckhardt stood in the doorway as the sheepish children found their seats. Except for Daniel. There he was, all alone with his great electric gizmo, looking guilty for everyone to see. Billy, evidently more scared than hurt, had the satisfied look of someone who was wronged but was about to witness justice.

Miss Eckhardt remained silent. She walked to her desk, looked at the children, and finally said softly, "Let's begin with the Lord's Prayer."

The daily routine began. First, the prayer, then the Bible reading, then the pledge of allegiance to the flag, and finally the children began singing "America." All the while, young Daniel was pondering his fate. He didn't have to wait much longer.

"*My country tis of thee, sweet land of liberty,*" the students began singing.

"All right," Miss Eckhardt said in a tone of voice that Daniel's mother used when he knew it wasn't all right. "Daniel will come with me to the cloakroom. Children, you will continue with the song."

4

Miss Eckhardt was so strict that students seldom misbehaved. But Daniel knew what the cloakroom meant. It meant a good whipping with a pecan switch. That, indeed, was his punishment. And even though Daniel was a strong boy, he was no match for the switch. His eyes were filled with tears when he went back to the classroom.

Daniel didn't know that Miss Eckhardt would view this as a major infraction. But, indeed, she did. For one week — five straight days — class began with a prayer, Bible reading, pledge, "America," and Daniel Moody being switched.

Daniel was growing up in a boy's paradise. School lasted less than six months and even with his dairy work, Daniel had plenty of free time. Running to the north of Taylor was the San Gabriel River, and to the south was Brushy Creek. Texas summers, which can last six months, were broken by endless hours at the fishing and swimming holes. The huge cypress trees along the banks of the San Gabriel provided great shade, and a long, lazy rope dangled over the cool river waters.

Downtown Taylor, with its railyards and thriving businesses, was always interesting. As Daniel grew up, he watched the horses and wagons come into town and heard about and finally saw the first of the new gasoline buggies. Telephones and electric lights, the most modern inventions of Daniel's childhood, made their way to Taylor while he was a boy.

In those days before movies, radio, and TV — all of which appeared later in the 20th century and were not part of Daniel's early years — public speaking was important and entertaining. And the best place to watch was at the courthouse. Daniel had four uncles who were lawyers, and he made many trips to nearby Georgetown, the county seat, to watch them in action. He particularly loved the criminal trials. Daniel would sit, fascinated, watching as the lawyers spoke colorfully and loudly, waving arms and pointing fingers as they passionately made their speeches to the juries.

Daniel did well in school, and he continued to work. He was soon old enough to drive the horse-drawn milk wagon, then he got a job at a coffee roasting plant in town, and finally he ended up learning electrical work. While still in high school, he began working as a meter reader and then an electrical lineman.

High school ended in the tenth grade. Daniel finished when he was fifteen. He wanted to go to college and planned to enroll at The University of Texas, located in Austin, only thirty miles southwest of his home.

One day, Daniel went to the university and knocked on the office door marked Dean of Admissions.

"Come in," the voice inside called.

Daniel opened the door. Inside, he saw stacks of books and papers spread throughout the small office. A man dressed in a suit was sitting at the desk, busily writing.

The man smiled. "Ah, you must be Mr. Moody."

Daniel was used to being called only Daniel. "Yes, sir."

"Well, I'm Dean Overstreet," he said as he shook Daniel's hand. "Please, have a seat. I've been looking over your application for admission to the University. You come from a well-educated family." The dean looked through the papers in front of him. "Four uncles are lawyers. Other family members are preachers and teachers. Your mother was a Latin teacher. I've heard of your father. Usually people call him Judge Moody."

"He was a cattle driver on the Chisholm Trail," explained Daniel. "He came to what they called Taylorsville as a claims agent with the railroad."

"Is he a lawyer?"

"No, he was Taylor's first mayor and later the justice of the peace."

"What does he do now?"

"Well, he makes a good living, but there's this business he invested in. See, it failed. His partner, who actually ran the business, left town, and my father vowed to pay every penny owed."

The dean looked troubled. "How are you going to pay for your education, Mr. Moody?"

"I've been working at odd jobs since I was ten."

The dean looked more troubled. "Why do you want an education?"

"Oh, I want to be a lawyer, like my uncles."

When Daniel returned home that evening, his mother was waiting on the front porch.

"Daniel, you look like you've lost your last friend in the world."

"They said I was too young, Mom. I can't go to college because I'm too young. If I can do the classwork, it shouldn't make any difference how old I am."

Mrs. Moody put her arm around her son's shoulders. "Do you remember that baseball game?"

"A couple of months ago?" Daniel's face lightened. "But that was kid stuff."

"You were the happiest kid I ever saw."

"Well, it's not every day you get to hit a game-winning homerun for your high school, Mom."

"That's right. But you have to keep remembering the good things so the bad things don't get you down. You still have your job with the electric company, don't you?"

"Yes. I wasn't going to give it up until I was accepted at the university."

"Well, it's a good job, and you've always liked electricity."

"Of course, you're always right, Mom. You know, I can buy my own tools with the money I saved for college. I can probably get my union card and be a full-time lineman. Maybe that will be better than college."

"We'll see about that later. In the meantime, enjoy your work as an electrician."

"No, I'm serious, Mom. If I'm not good enough for the university, I'll show them. I'll be an electrician."

"I quit."

The words caused V. D. Mann the manager of the Citizens Light and Power Company of Taylor, to look up from his paperwork. There in front of him stood a tall, lanky, red-headed teenager. Barely sixteen, Daniel Moody, loaded down with electrical tools, dripped with sweat from an already hot Texas morning.

"You can't quit, Moody. You've worked too hard to become an electrician. You've got your tools, your union card, and besides, you know electricity is becoming more and more important —"

"No, you have been very good to me, Mr. Mann. But it's a year since I finished high school, and I want to apply to the university again. If they take me I can become a lawyer like my uncles."

"I'm not even going to try . . . you are too headstrong to be talked out of anything. What made you make up your mind today?"

"Well, you see, sir, a few minutes ago I was sitting on top of a thirty-five-foot power pole, working with live electricity. Even at ten in the morning, the sun was already getting hot, and I knew it was only going to get worse. All of a sudden, I heard this woodpecker hammering away on a pecan tree."

"Okay, get to the point," Mr. Mann said. "What

does a woodpecker have to do with quitting your job?"

"Well, sir," Daniel said, "I figured if a bird could make a living with his head, so could I."

In 1910, at the age of sixteen, Daniel Moody was finally accepted at The University of Texas. He lived in Austin with an aunt and uncle and worked at odd jobs to make extra money. He raced his way through college and law school, and by 1914, he had completed his formal education. He had no money. Even the fee for his bar examination was beyond his reach, so he sold his one valuable possession — a gold watch — to pay for it. He passed his bar exam and returned to Taylor to start a law office with Harris Melasky, a childhood friend.

"Well, Harris, we certainly have it made now," said Daniel with a laugh. Harris joined his laughter as the two brand-new lawyers surveyed their surroundings.

Their "office" looked exactly like the insurance company storage closet it was. The young lawyers had cleaned it up and furnished it with two wooden packing crates for desks. A used typewriter was their only office equipment.

They managed to get some clients, and their legal careers began. One of Daniel's clients told him, "Your name, Daniel J. Moody, is too formal. People like an easy name, change it to Dan Moody." Daniel took the suggestion and was from then on he was known as Dan Moody.

The United States entered World War I in 1917. Dan attempted to enlist in the army but was rejected because his father had died in 1910, and Dan had to care for his sick mother. Dan was still able to enlist in the Texas National Guard. He rose from private to lieutenant, and set about organizing a company of

9

soldiers in Taylor for combat duty in Europe. He obtained the enlistments of enough men and led them to training camp in Arkansas. They were training when the war ended in 1918, and the troops were disbanded.

Dan returned to Taylor and continued his law practice. The years immediately after World War I were difficult for the United States. There was a feeling that things were changing too quickly. The automobile was starting to replace the horse, cities were growing, there were race riots in the large cities, and crime rates were rising. To make matters worse, the country's economic condition worsened, and by 1920 cotton prices had fallen to rock bottom. This was particularly devastating to Taylor, because its whole economy was based on cotton.

"Harris, I've been thinking about running for county attorney," Dan announced one day in 1920. "It's a part-time position, it would give me an office in the courthouse, and I could still keep my office in Taylor here with you. What do you think?"

"You're probably too young. Usually, that job goes to an older, more experienced lawyer."

"But I know I can do the job," said Dan. "It's not like district attorney, where I'd be prosecuting murders all the time. The county attorney only does the misdemeanors. I really want to try for it."

At age twenty-seven, Dan would be the youngest person ever to hold the office of county attorney. After talking with his friends and other lawyers, he decided to run.

Even at age twenty-seven, Dan had developed a good reputation with his fellow lawyers. They all decided that he would make a good county attorney, and no one else filed for the position. Dan was elected without opposition.

As Dan moved part of his office belongings into

his new courthouse office, he couldn't resist shutting the door and sitting at his new desk. He thought, "Dan Moody, the boy who used to watch his uncle try cases is now Dan Moody, County Attorney."

Not long after he became county attorney, Dan was working in his law office in Taylor.

"Mr. Moody," his secretary said as she cracked the door to his office. "There is a man here who wants to visit with you. He says it's a personal matter. His name is Roy Smith."

"Very well. Send him in."

The visitor had on conservative business attire — dark gray suit, neatly starched white shirt, and a dark tie. He had the look of a man who had a serious purpose, but he had a smile on his face.

Dan rose to greet him.

As the visitor shook Dan's hand warmly, he began talking, "Mr. Moody, thank you for seeing me. I'm Roy Smith, and I have something very important to discuss with you. You see, I'm what we call a kleagle, and it's my job to find one hundred percent *white* Americans to organize local chapters of the Invisible Empire, the Knights of the Ku Klux Klan."

2

Terror Comes to Texas

"We are different than any other organization in town, Mr. Moody," Roy Smith explained. "Our secret membership allows us to take real action to clean up our towns, to get rid of the bums, prostitutes, gamblers, bootleggers, and habitual criminals — the ones who are tearing our society down."

Smith spent the next few minutes recalling the history of the Klan. It was originally organized after the Civil War to fight carpetbaggers and scalawags and protect decent people in the South. Colonel William Simmons of Atlanta revived it in 1915 as a secret lodge of men to deal with what he saw as a new crisis that threatened America. Smith said that this crisis was blacks and the influx of foreigners — particularly, Jews and Catholics — who didn't act like regular Americans. Smith felt the Klan was very patriotic and against crime.

Smith explained how the Klan first organized in Texas. "Our Mr. Upchurch arrived in Houston this past October for the reunion of Confederate soldiers. Within a week, a chapter had been chartered. We had a cross-burning ceremony outside of town in Bellaire and immediately began helping to clean up the town. Texans are excited about our ideas, Mr. Moody. Within a few months, we had a hundred Klan chapters from

Beaumont to El Paso. And, this is the really exciting part, if I can find a hundred good men here in Taylor to join, you will be Klan No. 117. I've never left a town yet where I couldn't find those hundred good men."

Dan's thoughts were racing. He hadn't heard much about the Klan, but what he'd heard was bad. What they said about crime might be true, it was out of control, but their way of "helping" the police was to take the law into their own hands. What that usually meant was a severe flogging to whomever didn't agree with them. They preached law and order, but to Dan, their brand of justice was to violate the law and create disorder. As a lawyer and county attorney, they went against everything Dan believed.

But Dan was also aware that the Klan's ideas were very popular. He chose his words carefully. "Mr. Smith, I must tell you that your anti-crime message sounds like one of my own speeches. But I'm very concerned about these reports that the Klan supports flogging."

"I'm not going to be shy with you," Smith replied. "The Klan does not support lawlessness, but many of our members know the only way to get the message to these lawbreakers. You visit with them, and you give them fair warning to clear out of town. But if they keep up their activities . . . Well, a good whipping gets the message across loud and clear."

Dan could scarcely believe what he was hearing. The time for careful words was over. The Klan might be very popular, but Dan Moody would not be part of it.

"Mr. Smith, I can't believe that you would pro-pose such an idea to a county attorney. You have nothing to do with law and order and nothing to do with Americanism. This country was founded on laws, due process, and orderly procedures to enforce our laws. What you propose is lawlessness. Every man could be his own judge and jury. Why, that's

13

nothing but anarchy!" Dan rose and escorted Smith to the door.

"I'm shocked at your attitude." Smith remained very businesslike. "There are judges, preachers, bankers, businessmen, and everyday working people all over the state who have heard our message and joined. When I told you how we fight crime, I thought you would say 'Halleluia.'"

"There will be no 'Halleluias' for the Klan from Dan Moody. The people of Taylor have no use for your gang of bed-sheeted vigilantes." Dan opened the outer door to the street and handed Smith his hat.

Smith stepped out to the street, gave his tie a slight tug to straighten it, placed his hat on his head, and looked straight at Dan. "Oh, don't worry. We will have more than enough members. We will be having our first cross burning within the week." With that, Smith turned and walked confidently down the street.

Barely a week had passed when Dan Moody drove his Ford sedan to the hardware store in downtown Taylor. While Dan had not become rich as a lawyer, his county attorney job and law firm in Taylor brought him a good living. He was particularly proud of his shiny new black Ford. It allowed him to get to the courthouse in Georgetown in less than an hour.

As he got out of his car, he saw Jim Salter, a childhood friend who was two years older. Jim was a smart businessman who was working hard selling oil field equipment.

"Good afternoon, Dan." Jim was dressed in a business suit with tie and hat.

"Good to see you," Dan said.

"Could I have a word with you? Perhaps across the street under a tree?" Jim looked down the street to the trees around the town hall square. It was a fine spring afternoon, but in their suits the sun would soon have both men sweating.

14

As the two men walked, they discussed weather, family, and friends.

Arriving under the shade of a pecan tree, Jim stopped. "I wanted to get into the shade, but I also wanted to get off the sidewalk so we could have some privacy." He leaned toward Dan. "You see, two days ago I joined the Ku Klux Klan. We had our first meeting last night. Burned a cross and everything."

A worried look crossed Dan's face. "Why are you telling me? Isn't it a secret society?"

"Not with me, it isn't. I guess I was duped by all their talk about law and order. I paid the money — ten dollars for initiation and six-fifty for the robe and hood — and even took the oath."

"What turned you around so quickly?"

"You did," Jim replied. "It seems right after the oath, the first order of business was a speech by the kleagle from Houston, somebody named Smith. Smith starts yelling about bootleggers and gamblers, and before you know it, he says you're the worst of the lot. Called you by name. Said our 'so-called county attorney is the criminal's best friend.' When I heard that you were against the Klan and listened to that lying kleagle call you a friend of criminals, I knew this wasn't for me."

"I appreciate your faith in me —"

"Wait, there's more. The crowd, there must have been a hundred and twenty men there, was lathered up by the kleagle. What with the cross burning, their new robes, the ceremony, singing the national anthem and all, they were cheering and hurrahing at every sentence he said. Including when he said getting a good man to run for county attorney against you was a top priority."

Dan didn't pause as he responded. "I appreciate the information. But I didn't work this hard to be a lawyer and county attorney to be frightened by a loudmouth in a bed sheet. I don't think they can find a lawyer in Williamson County to run against me, so maybe I'll run for district attorney."

"District attorney?"

"Sure. That covers both Travis and Williamson counties. See, it will give them more lawyers to find someone to run against me."

"You aren't taking me seriously," said Jim.

"Oh, I am. But I'm not going to be frightened, and I *am* going to run for D.A. I want to prosecute the more serious crimes, and Ben Robertson probably isn't going to run for re-election as D.A. anyway."

"Well, maybe you will run for it, but it won't hurt to keep your plans a secret," advised Jim.

"That's good advice. Thank you. But I won't be taking it. I'm going to pay a visit on our local Klan leader and let him know. I think I'll do it right now." Dan began walking back towards his Ford.

"Stop it right now!" exclaimed Jim. "This Klan thing is serious. Those one hundred and twenty men last night are your neighbors. Even under the robes, I know from their autos and shoes most everyone there. They are regular people, but they change when they have those robes on. Oh, I can tell from that look on your face I'm making you more determined. But, Dan, promise me you'll be careful."

A slightly calmed Dan Moody murmured a reply.

"Oh, before I forget. Let me give you this pamphlet they give new Klansmen." Jim held out some papers. "You might find it helpful someday."

"Political suicide," was the greeting Sheriff Lee Allen used to announce his presence in the county attorney's office.

Dan Moody looked up from his desk in the county courthouse in time to see the sheriff walk through the open doorway and take a seat. Uninvited, as usual.

Sheriff Allen was a handsome young law officer, barely older than Dan, but already with nine years' experience as the county sheriff. Lee was a good lawman and a good politician. He could charm the grandmothers at a church picnic then turn right around and talk a hardened criminal into surrendering.

Lee's office was also in the courthouse, and he was a frequent visitor to Dan's. Dan often asked Lee for advice about politics, law enforcement, and human nature.

"Political suicide. That's what you call it when you run the Klan organizer out of your office and then go to the head of the Klan and challenge him to run someone against you. Not only for your current office, but you're already running for a higher office." Lee's smile made it clear he was having fun teasing his friend.

"Where did you hear all this?"

"Hear it! Hear it! You'd have to be a blind, deaf hermit not to know about it. It's the talk of the county. Talk of *two* counties."

"So where does the Williamson County sheriff stand on the Klan?" Dan asked.

"You know where I stand. I'm a hundred percent behind you. Sometimes I wish you'd pick your battles a little more carefully and maybe after we talked first."

"Good advice, sheriff. I'll slow down a little next time. How is the county reacting?"

" 'Bout half and half, I guess. Half don't have much use for the Klan and half figure you'll come to your senses and see that they really are on your side. But that could change. There's a lot of frustrated people out there that want the bootleggers out of business. And then there's cotton farmers who lost everything and need someone to blame."

"What do you really know for sure about the Klan?" Dan asked.

17

"Not very much, until a few days ago. But then there was their show over by Shiloh. Everyone in east Williamson County knows how much the Widow Jones needs help with those seven young'uns she's raising."

That Sunday, ten men with Klan robes had burst into the worship service at the Baptist church near Shiloh. They marched up to the pulpit, presented the preacher with an envelope full of cash, and said he should use it to help the Widow Jones. Then they led the congregation, singing "Onward Christian Soldiers," and the Klansmen marched back out.

Dan agreed. "There isn't a more deserving lady."

"The Klan made a lot of friends with that. And the church members spread the news faster than any newspaper."

"So all everyone hears is the flashy charity work. Maybe they parade through downtown in their bed sheets, burn a cross or two," Dan said with a frown.

"Oh, the parades, they do that all over. Then they get bored and start with the tar parties."

Dan's eyes widened. "Do you know that for sure? I've heard stories, but—"

"I made some phone calls around the state this morning," interrupted Lee. "What they do is, they pick a suspected bootlegger, beat him, tar and feather him, and then order him out of town."

"Well, the bootleggers—"

"What about this? They went after a lawyer in Houston who was defending too many criminals. They went after a black bellhop at the fanciest hotel in Dallas. They went after a gambler in Fort Worth. There have been dozens of these tar parties around the state."

"And what's being done?"

"Nothing. Not one thing," said Lee. "The local officers might go through the motions of an investigation. But everyone in town knows who the suspects are, and no one gets arrested. My suspicions are a lot of local police and deputies are either in the Klan or happy for the help."

"I can't believe it. How can someone sworn to uphold the law be able to tolerate the Klan?"

"Well, you better believe it. One sheriff I talked to insisted he wasn't a member, but he told me flat out that the Klan never tarred and feathered a man that didn't deserve it. And you don't have to look too far to find worse." Lee ticked them off on his fingers. "Travis County sheriff admits he's a member, at least in private. Everyone says the Austin police commissioner is too. And let's not forget our own police commissioner in Taylor. If he hasn't joined yet, you and I would both be surprised."

Dan sat in silence for a minute. "Well, there is nothing we can do about the Klan here as long as they obey the law. Maybe we'll be lucky, and our local members will be content to have their meetings and burn their crosses."

"That's a pretty thought, Dan, but don't bet the house on it," said Lee.

"Gentlemen," said George Wheeler. "Tonight we are going to start a new phase of our activities." The men gathered around Wheeler on the street in front of the Austin Ku Klux Klan hall. It was on San Jacinto Street, downtown above a dry goods store. The weekly Klan meeting had finished, and Wheeler was talking with eight men who stayed behind.

"We've had enough of parades and picnics. It's time for action," continued Wheeler. He had grown up near Austin, and he didn't like it at all the way Austin had changed from when he was a boy. "We left a warning notice at the capitol last week. We left a notice on Congress Avenue the week before. The newspaper reported both notices, so everyone knows of our intentions."

"Chester Birmingham. He's a Negro, and he's got lots of money. Always acting better than he is."

"Where would a Negro get money?" asked one of the men.

"My point exactly." When he was a boy, Wheeler had never heard of a Negro with money. It wasn't allowed. The men, Wheeler's father and his friends, wouldn't ever have let it happen. In their minds it wasn't right that Negroes had money when decent white folks went hungry.

"Ol' Chester must be gambling or bootlegging or something," said Wheeler. Then he outlined his plan. "I know for a fact that Chester will be out near Manor later tonight. I grew up out that way, and I know the area well. I know exactly where we can catch him. Let's let Mr. Chester Birmingham have a taste of the justice of the Invisible Empire."

Wheeler and his men drove off into the night. He had scouted Chester and his activities well. Chester was visiting his grandmother's home. He would eat dinner there, visit for awhile, and then walk two blocks to his sister's house.

Wheeler and his robed, masked group hid in the bushes along the route. Chester, creature of habit, did not disappoint them. He happened along fifteen minutes after they took their positions.

The hooded men were on Chester before he knew what had happened. Chester struggled, but he was no match for the strong, young men Wheeler had brought. They quickly controlled him, a man pulling each wrist and ankle in a different direction. They stretched Chester out, face down, dangling and writhing in the air.

The others ripped off Chester's sweaty shirt and began the whipping from the side. Each lash from the strap of leather cut deeply across Chester's back. The white-robed Klansmen showed no mercy and continued to take turns, lash after lash. After awhile, they dropped Chester to the ground, bloody and too weak to do more than twist and moan. Then the four who had been holding him got their licks in. As the strap fell again and again, the men taunted Chester. Chester didn't even hear them.

Finally, Wheeler gave a signal, and two men went to his automobile. Each dragged back a small tub of warm tar. With some help, they lifted the tubs and carefully poured the oozing tar onto Chester, who moaned. Wheeler then reached inside his blood-spattered robe and produced a burlap sack of chicken feathers, which he waggled empty onto Chester.

"This is your warning, Chester!" yelled Wheeler as he stood over the feather-coated body. He had to wave away the wispy little feathers still wafting in the air.

"The Invisible Empire will not tolerate your kind. You pack your bags and you leave this town!" That's how it should be, Wheeler believed, when decent white men took responsibility. "You hear me, boy?"

With that, Wheeler and his gang took their tar tubs and their slick, shiny leather strap and retreated into the darkness.

Sheriff Lee Allen saw the young county attorney walking from the courthouse to his car. Dan Moody had completed some routine cases and was heading back to his office in Taylor. Lee called out and greeted his friend in their customary manner.

"I suppose you seen the *Austin American* from this morning?" Lee caught up and walked beside Dan.

"No, I haven't read the newspaper, but if you're referring to the Klan incident, I certainly have heard about it. It was the talk of all the legal eagles at the courthouse today."

"Manor's what, ten or so miles south of the county line? So it's not in our jurisdiction. But with

21

the violence that close, our own Klan will be aching for action soon."

"Maybe not."

"Dan, there's been a story about Klan violence on the front page of the *Austin American* nearly every day this month. Not only Texas, but the whole country's going crazy. It seems like the Klan's about taken over in Oklahoma."

"Maybe all the attention the Klan got this past month will force people to take a second look at their tactics." When they got to his Ford, Dan tossed his briefcase onto the front passenger seat.

"Well, don't look for the Texas Legislature to take a stand against them," replied Lee. "I was in Austin this morning. Wright Patman had the courage to introduce a resolution opposing the Klan, and the House voted right after lunch not to consider his resolution. Even Governor Neff doesn't seem to want to wrassle them directly."

"We have to hope our boys know to stay within the law here in Williamson County."

"Unless you get elected district attorney," Lee said, "and then you'll have both counties to worry about."

After saying goodbye, Dan began the drive back to Taylor. The speed limit was 23 miles per hour, but until the road got paved it was difficult to go even that fast. Dan enjoyed the long drive. He looked to his right across the San Gabriel River.

He recalled how he fished and swam there when he was growing up. He recalled the trips to the courthouse to watch his uncles practice law. Now, here he was, Williamson County's youngest county attorney ever and, if he was successful, soon to be the youngest district attorney ever. Then he recalled how Miss Eckhardt had whacked him with a pecan switch. That was a lot different from what the Klan had done to

Chester Birmingham down in Manor yesterday. For sure, Dan knew which one hurt worse and which one needed to be accounted for in a court of law.

Some days Dan Moody wished he was still a boy with nothing more important on his mind than fishing.

Dan worked hard for the next two years. The respect of his fellow lawyers allowed him to run unopposed for district attorney. Sometimes he thought maybe they were so smart they didn't want the job. The Klan's plan to find an opponent for Dan turned out to be nothing but an empty threat. The incumbent district attorney, partly out of frustration with his inability to stop the Klan violence in Austin, quit his job in late April 1922. Governor Neff appointed Dan district attorney effective May 1, 1922. He was twenty-eight years old.

The Klan's empty threat to defeat Dan was about their only setback during those years. The Ku Klux Klan gained strength, not only in Texas, but nationwide. Their political strength grew as they won election after election, and their reign of vigilante terror continued. There were few arrests and no convictions.

It seemed no one could stop the Klan. No one could stop the hate, and no one could stop the violence. No one except Dan Moody.

3

The klan Delivers a Warning

There was only a slight chill in the air that January evening in 1923. As winters in central Texas went, it was the norm. Warm days reached to the 70's or 80's, until a coldfront blew in and dropped nighttime temperatures slightly below freezing for a couple of days. Gradually, the air warmed again until the next cold front came along. Only a true blue norther, a front that came along perhaps once or twice a year, would produce snow or ice or anything that really resembled winter.

Normally, a Monday night in January would find Georgetown a sleepy town nestled along the San Gabriel River. But tonight, the pasture along the banks of the south fork of the San Gabriel, right on the outskirts of town, was rapidly filling with cars. Men from town, along with farmers and residents of nearby communities, came in twos and threes. They did not linger long in the pasture. Each carried a bundle into the nearby building.

The building had originally been built as a barn, but two years earlier had been adapted to its current purpose. With some electrical wiring and a few alterations, it made a perfect meeting hall for the new organization. It held nearly two hundred men, and its isolated location — out in a pasture, a river protecting its flank, but barely one mile from the county court-house — made it perfect for the secret organization.

The building was the Klavern, the official indoors meeting place of Georgetown Klan No. 178. When there were crosses to burn, the adjacent pasture made an excellent spot for the ceremony.

Tonight, the men were hurrying into the Klavern because they had elected new officers. Dr. John Martin was the new Exalted Cyclops, the local head of the Klan chapter, and he had arranged for a special speaker, Reverend A. A. Davis. Although a very young man, Davis had built a reputation as a fiery speaker, a strict moral crusader, and a man of action. None of the Klansmen wanted to be late.

Once inside the Klavern, the Klansmen put on their official Klan robes. Even though a bed sheet would indeed do in a pinch, the men wore simple white robes that they purchased when they joined the Klan. They placed the hoods over their faces and found a seat in the crowded Klavern.

Dr. John Martin, in full Klan regalia, sat on a small platform at the front of the Klavern. Seated with him were the four other members of Klan No. 178's executive committee, or Klokann: the Klaliff, vice president, the Kligrapp, secretary, the Klabee, treasurer, and the Kludd, chaplain.

The sixth man seated at the front was Reverend Davis. There was a lectern to speak from, and on the table next to the lectern lay a Bible, a gavel, and the Kloran, the official ritual book of the Klan.

The Exalted Cyclops, Dr. Martin, rose from his seat and reached for the gavel. The Klansmen became quiet even before he pounded the gavel on the lectern to begin the meeting.

As Dr. Martin looked out on the sea of robed men, he began, "Greetings, fellow citizens of the Invisible Empire. The sentries are posted outside, and this

Konklave is officially called to order. I will recognize our Kludd to begin our meeting with a prayer."

The Kludd rose and delivered a typical Klan prayer, asking for the Almighty to preserve the white race, make America strong, and make all evil-doers tremble at the thought of the Ku Klux Klan. As he finished the prayer, two men, K. C. Baker and Cornelius Beard, arrived late from the nearby community of Weir. Finding no seats, they stood in the back of the Klavern.

The Exalted Cyclops returned to the lectern and led the men in singing "Onward Christian Soldiers." He then began his introduction of the guest speaker.

"Citizens," he began. All Klansmen were "citizens" of the Invisible Empire. The initiation ceremony was officially called a naturalization when a Klansman left the world of the aliens and became a citizen. "Tonight we will dispense with our usual business so that we will have plenty of time to hear our speaker. Reverend A. A. Davis is known throughout the state as a fine orator. He can tell you the real truth about Rome and its threat to America. Mark his words well. These Catholics owe their allegiance to the Pope in Rome, not to the stars and stripes. I give you Reverend A. A. Davis."

The Klavern erupted with applause and cheers. While nearly every Klansman present knew a local family or two who were of the Catholic faith and knew them to be good neighbors, it made no difference. Once they put on their robes, the Klansmen were ready to believe anything as long as it came packaged in the traditional values of God, America, and law and order.

"Fellow Klansmen, I have come to give a grave warning about a plot by the Pope in Rome to take over America," the Reverend A. A. Davis began. He spoke for an hour. His message covered all the half-truths and outright lies the Klan had devised about the Catholic church. Davis was a very effective speaker. He was interrupted frequently by cheers and applause but also had the men completely quiet and near tears as he described in great detail crimes committed by Catholics against children. But most of his anger was directed at the Pope.

He concluded, "The Roman Pope's plot to make America a province of Rome will be stopped. It will be stopped by our fiery crosses, by you citizens of the Invisible Empire."

The Klavern burst into a frenzy, united in their hatred for the Pope and their desire to protect America.

The next day most of those men would return to their regular lives and greet and do business with their friends and neighbors who were Catholics and foreign-born and blacks and Jews. Normalcy and common sense would return to their lives. But tonight, as a robed brotherhood, cloaked in the mystic and secret ways of the Klan, they hated.

Exalted Cyclops Martin rose to the lectern. He thanked Reverend Davis for his fine speech and then explained, "We do have a short business meeting to conduct, citizens."

The robed men were not in the mood for a business meeting, but they finally calmed down enough to listen to the Klabee give the financial report. The Klabee was reminding the men that their annual dues needed to be paid when Cornelius Beard, one of the men who arrived late from Weir, called out, "We have more important business than this. Let's hear from K. C. Baker." He then turned to his friend. "Come on, K. C., tell them what you were telling me," he urged.

K. C. stepped forward as all of the Klansmen shifted to see the back of the hall. K.C. was the barber in Weir, and he was a large man, tall and built more like a blacksmith than a barber.

"It's this fella, Burleson. He's up in Weir, staying at a widow's boarding house. It's more than staying, it's adultery going on in that house. It's a disgrace," K. C. explained as his voice grew louder.

The barber then looked directly towards the Exalted Cyclops and demanded, "I want to know what we are going to do about it."

"Yeah," cried another man. "Let's have some action on it." The crowd was becoming loud in general agreement that something needed to be done when Dr. Martin beat his gavel forcefully and repeatedly to bring order.

"Now, we will have none of this at our Klavern," Dr. Martin stated.

The Georgetown Klan had not been involved in vigilante violence, and Dr. Martin intended it to stay that way. Dr. Martin had joined the Klan to preserve America, do charitable acts, and help the authorities fight crime. He was not interested in vigilante violence. While the men respected Dr. Martin, there was a good deal of grumbling and agitation among the robed figures. It was then that Reverend Davis stood, held up both his hands, and reassured them, "Don't worry. I'll see about this. Go back to your meeting."

The Klansmen settled down, and the Klabee finished his financial report. The Exalted Cyclops led the men in singing "The Old Rugged Cross." He then recognized the Kludd to conclude the meeting.

The Kludd went to the lectern. He turned to Reverend Davis. "Would you join me, Reverend? It would be an honor." The two preachers then led the men in the Kloxology, the religious song, distorted for Klan purposes, that always closed the Konklave.

The Klavern cleared slowly after the meeting. Several Klansmen went up to the front to shake

Reverend Davis' hand. Enjoying their praise and congratulations, Davis was one of the last to leave the Klavern.

Usually, Davis traveled by train and stayed at each stop with a local host, who also drove him around. In Georgetown, that honor went to Norman Robertson, who walked beside Davis toward his automobile. There were only a few cars scattered around the pasture. As the two men removed their robes, Robertson warned the preacher, "Be careful, there's a stand of cactus in front of you."

Two men approached them. "Reverend Davis, I'm K. C. Baker," announced one. K.C. and his friend Beard had waited patiently for Davis since the end of the meeting.

"Ah, yes, Mr. Baker. I'm glad you remained," said Davis.

The four men introduced themselves and were joined by John McDaniel, a student at the local college, Southwestern. McDaniel, on sentry duty that night, had remained outside the hall during the meeting.

Davis turned to Baker. "Tell us all the details of this problem."

Baker began to recount how Mrs. Campbell, a widow in her thirties, ran a boarding house in Weir to support herself and her children.

"As far as we knew, it was a respectable boarding house until this Burleson started staying there. At first he stayed for a few days at a time but now his stays are for weeks. He's a traveling salesman for a hosiery outfit in Indianapolis. But he sure doesn't do much traveling," concluded Baker.

"I suppose he hasn't admitted it?" asked Davis.

"Of course not," interjected Beard. "His kind never would. But tell him the rest, K.C."

"Well, last week, Burleson came by my barbershop. He said he didn't appreciate me talking about him and Mrs. Campbell. He said I was nothing but a big, fat, stupid gossip and threatened to give me a whipping if I ever talked about him and Mrs. Campbell again."

"It's a disgrace," Beard added, "that a man with loose morals can be threatening a Klansman."

"Let's think about this," said Davis. "It certainly looks bad for this Burleson fellow, but I don't suppose we have certain proof."

"No, I haven't broken down the door to take a picture or anything," Baker said.

"I don't suppose we need proof," Davis said. "I think I'll pay him a visit and give him a warning to move out. If he's not doing anything wrong, he ought to take our warning and stay somewhere else."

McDaniel, the college student, spoke eagerly, "If you need help, I'll go along,"

"That's what we need," said Davis. "I'll take you and one other fellow. We can borrow a car and all go out to visit this Burleson fellow tomorrow. I will say this, men. I've made many such visits, and I've always had success. These immoral types, these gamblers, bootleggers, and adulterers, they know the Klan means business."

K. C. Baker praised Reverend Davis. "I knew you were a man of action. Our so-called Cyclops wants nothing to do but talk, talk, talk. Action is what we need."

The men concluded the arrangements for the next day. They then got into their cars and drove off into the night.

Tuesday morning began as a sunny spring day. The chill of the night evaporated as the sun rose and began to heat the air. Reverend Davis made a few greetings around town, conducted some business, and by mid-morning was ready for his trip to Weir.

30

He borrowed a car from his friend, S.J. Purl. Another man, a Klansman and friend of Robertson, met him at Purl's house. The two of them drove to the corner of Pine and University, where McDaniel was waiting for them. The three then drove the short distance to Weir.

In 1923 Weir was a small but thriving community only a few miles northeast of Georgetown along the San Gabriel River. While its thousand residents made it barely one-fifth the size of Georgetown, its prosperous Main Street featured two banks and several stores.

As the Klansmen drove into Weir that morning, everything appeared normal. Business was being conducted, school was in session, and everyone seemed to be enjoying the sunshine. The Klansmen wore their normal workday clothes and did not stand out from the other people.

None of the men knew exactly where K. C.'s barbershop was located, but after driving around they decided to stop at Joiner's drugstore to ask directions. All three men left the car and entered the drugstore.

"Good morning," called Mr. Joiner as they entered the store.

They all responded warmly. Davis then walked over to the druggist. "Davis, Reverend A. A. Davis is the name," he said as the two men shook hands. "We're not from here, and I need some directions to the barbershop."

Joiner let out a small chuckle. "Well, K. C. has the only barbershop in town, so I guess he doesn't need much of a sign. But he's my next-door neighbor. His shop is the next one over towards the bank."

"So we almost found it by accident." Davis smiled. "Thanks for your neighborliness. We need a brief visit with K. C."

A short while later, K. C. Baker wore a look of pleasant surprise on his face as the three men entered his barbershop.

"Well, when you want action, Reverend A. A. Davis is your man," announced Baker to the man in the chair and the one customer waiting.

"Good morning," said Davis.

"Yes, sir, action. That's what we need. A man to shake up the sinners around here," bellowed Baker.

"Keep your voice down, K. C.," said Davis.

"Oh, don't worry. We're all Klansmen here," said Baker. His two customers nodded agreement.

"Well, we won't trouble you for long, K. C. We only stopped by for directions."

Baker took Davis to the front window of his shop and gave him easy directions. The Campbell house was a short distance away. Then Baker asked in a voice barely above a whisper, "Oh, Reverend, where is your robe and hood and — ?"

"No need for them. We are only going to pay a visit," said Davis. "And no need for you. You've made a splendid contribution. I've found this next part works best if the message comes from strangers."

Baker continued in his whisper, "You must have heard that the sheriff and D.A. are no friends of the Klan —"

"Don't worry. These moral wrongdoers like Burleson are all a bunch of cowards. After I warn him, he'll be packing his bags and out of town by sundown." Davis broke away and opened the door. "Good day, gentlemen." He waved as he and his party began to leave.

The three men got into the borrowed automobile, and McDaniel drove the few blocks to the Campbell house as Davis gave directions.

"There it is," called out Reverend Davis as they turned the corner.

"This must be our lucky day," said McDaniel. "That looks to be him in the front yard."

The Campbell boarding house was a well kept, two-story, white frame house with black shutters on the windows. A large yard surrounded it. The white picket fence had a gate at the front sidewalk.

As McDaniel pulled over, the man in the front yard didn't seem to notice and proceeded to walk back toward the house.

"Burleson!" shouted Davis. "You need to come here!"

The man seemed startled at hearing his name called.

"I need to have a word with you," Davis called in a slightly lower voice.

The man came near to the open back window from which Davis had called out. As the man got close to the window, Davis asked, "You are Robert Burleson?"

The man nodded yes.

"We're from the local chapter of the Ku Klux Klan. Your immorality has come to our attention. You are a disgrace, and your kind will not be tolerated."

"Now see here, man," Burleson interrupted. "You must have been talking to that blowhard, Baker."

Davis, his face rapidly turning red, responded with a stern voice. "No, you see here. You are living in adultery, and you must stop. Don't disobey the Klan. Our justice is swift and sure." Davis handed Burleson an envelope. "This is your only warning. Heed it, sir. Heed our warning." Davis nodded to McDaniel, who immediately began to drive off.

Burleson, caught by surprise, had taken the envelope but the car left before he could think of what to reply. He stood in front of the house, envelope in hand, thoroughly frustrated. He grew madder by the second as he walked into the house.

"What was all that about?" called Fannie Campbell.

"You better come and see," Burleson called back from the front parlor.

As Fannie entered the parlor, she could tell something was wrong. Fannie was an attractive woman who did not look like she could be the mother of five children. After her husband had died four years earlier, she sold the farm, moved into town, and rented some of the rooms in her large house to earn extra money. She lived off the interest from the money the farm had brought. Her three boys, aged ten, fourteen, and seventeen, also worked to support the family. It wasn't easy, but Fannie somehow managed.

Burleson held the envelope up. "It seems I have come to the attention of the local Klan boys."

"The who?"

"The Klan, you know, the Ku Klux Klan, champions of the downtrodden and widows," said Burleson sarcastically.

"And what would the Klan have to do with you?" demanded Fannie.

"Not me, us," emphasized Burleson. "They have accused us of living in adultery."

"That's silly," replied Fannie. "Where would they get such an idea?"

"I should have told you. But K. C. Baker has been shooting his mouth —"

"K. C. Baker!" exclaimed Fannie. "Why, he's the biggest gossip in town. Everyone regards him as a fat, old fool."

"Which, indeed, he is," replied Burleson. "But when he's not being a fat fool, my guess is he puts on his white sheet and heads to Georgetown every Monday night to be with all the other fools."

Fannie and Burleson stopped and looked at each other. "Fools or not, the Klan can be serious," said Fannie. "What's in the envelope?"

Burleson opened the plain, unmarked envelope. The paper inside bore the letterhead of Georgetown Klan 178. The Ku Klux Klan seal was at the bottom. They both read the typewritten words silently:

ADULTERY!!
YOU HAVE SINNED AND MUST LEAVE TOWN.
DO IT NOW!

Burleson crumpled the note into a ball and threw it against the wall. "I'll kill him! That idiot Baker has been an idiot long enough."

Fannie grabbed Burleson with both arms. "Calm down."

As Burleson looked down, he saw tears streaming down Fannie's face. They stood silently.

At last Fannie grabbed the crumpled note and dashed to the kitchen. As Burleson caught up with her, he saw the letter burning up in the stove.

"So much for the Klan," Fannie said. "If I could survive Charly's death, sell the farm, and raise my family by myself, I think I'm strong enough to handle this," she said with determination. "But Robert, I want you to promise you won't give K. C. Baker the thrashing he deserves. Let this silliness blow over."

"I'll promise you that, but I'm not sure it'll blow over. We need to be extra careful, especially at night," said Burleson.

"Well, I have two nearly full-grown teenage boys to protect me," said Fannie. "I only use my shotgun for rattlesnakes. But I reckon if some men with sheets on came around the house, I'd give them the same thing a snake gets."

The following morning, Burleson began his workday in Georgetown. He had business to conduct on the square before he went to call on several customers in Taylor. He had finished his Georgetown business and was returning to his car when he spied a man down the street on the corner by Miles'

Laundry. There, talking to three other men, was the man who had threatened him the day before. He could scarcely believe his eyes.

As he strode to the corner, he recalled his promise to Fannie. Well, that was only not to thrash *Baker*. This was another matter entirely.

Burleson approached the four men talking on the corner. "So, we meet again," he yelled. "I believe we have a conversation to finish."

"Who are you?" Davis placed his hands in front of him defensively.

"Don't give me that. You knew full well who I was yesterday."

"Well, do you have an eyewitness?"

"You know darn well, there was no one else around. Except you and your fellow Klansmen."

Davis spoke with a sincere even soft voice. "Son, you don't have an eyewitness, and I'm a preacher. Name's Reverend A. A. Davis. I have never met you before, and I know nothing about any conversation."

"You were in Weir yesterday."

"Weir? Where's that? I've never been to any Weir." Davis smiled politely. "You simply must have mistaken me for someone else."

"You know darn well you were in Weir yesterday," insisted Burleson.

"No, sir, it wasn't me." Davis looked him square in the eye and lied with a sincerity that could convince anyone. "I have an appointment to keep, sir. I'll be on my way." Davis and the others walked off as Burleson found himself alone on the corner.

Burleson again found himself speechless. Perhaps he was mistaken, but he didn't think so. He had seen the man close up yesterday, and the voice was identical. Well, perhaps the Klan wasn't so tough when people stood up to them.

Burleson drove to Taylor and spent the afternoon

calling on customers, taking orders for more socks. He greeted many of his acquaintances on the streets. Late that afternoon, he told the story of the Klan's threats to a group of six men along Main Street. One of them mentioned that the Klan was not used to having its warnings go unheeded.

"The Klan doesn't scare me. They are a bunch of blowhards." As Burleson told the story, he became bolder and bolder. "Cowards. I'll kill the first twenty-one I see."

4

"The Worst Beat Man I Ever Saw!"

"What a wonderful message our preacher had today!" exclaimed Mary Moody as she and her brother walked out of church together.

"Easter is always a special service," observed Dan Moody.

Since becoming district attorney, Dan had moved to Austin where his office was. But he frequently returned to Taylor to visit his sister and friends. Since both their parents had died, and Dan was not married, he and his sister became an even closer family.

"What a gorgeous day!" Mary exclaimed as the two emerged into the sunlight.

Central Texas spring was the best season of the year. Days were warm, not hot and humid as they were in the summer. Wildflowers covered the countryside. There would be an infinite variety of such flowers. Bluebonnets, Indian paint brushes, and black-eyed Susans would transform dead, gray winter fields into bright palettes of blue, red, and yellow.

"Dan, I have to rush home. There is a lot to do to get dinner on the table," Mary said. The extended family would be gathering after church for the feast that Mary and her aunts and cousins were preparing.

Dan stayed in front of the church, visiting with friends. The whole town of Taylor was proud of Dan. As district attorney of the two-county area, Travis and Williamson, he was kept very busy. The city of Austin had grown in population to more than 50,000 people. With all the activities generated by the state capitol and university, it needed a full-time district attorney of its own. But Dan also had to travel frequently to Georgetown to handle Williamson County cases. That left Dan with little time for anything other than work, so today would be a well deserved day off for him.

"Dan, I just wanted to tell you what a good job you are doing," one man told him as he patted him on the back.

"You'll always have my vote," added another man. Even on his day off, Dan had to remember he held a political office.

Dan visited in front of the church until nearly everyone had left. He then began to walk the few blocks to his family home, where Mary and the others would be preparing the supper, and the rest of the family would be gathering.

Dan walked slowly and enjoyed the beautiful spring day. He had been district attorney for nearly a year now and was growing more comfortable with the job. He had been successful with his trials, and the public seemed to appreciate his work. He had not really focused on his future but could see himself being district attorney for quite a while.

As the Moodys were sitting down to their mid-afternoon meal in Taylor, Fannie Campbell, over in Weir, was finishing washing the dishes from her family's Easter meal. She had already had a full day. She and her five children had been up early and had gone to church services at the Methodist church, where she had taught her regular Sunday School class.

It had been over two months since the note had

39

been delivered by the Klan. While she had been frightened at first and had many sleepless nights, she no longer worried about it. Besides, she was moving back to Seguin where her parents lived. She had completed the sale of the house on Saturday, but she would be allowed to live there for a few weeks while she made arrangements for the move.

She had been working hard, and now she wanted to rest for the remainder of the day. She had asked Carrie Jones, her sister-in-law, to come by so they could visit Charly's grave. Mr. Burleson had been kind enough to agree to drive them out to the cemetery, but he seemed more interested in having a pleasant drive in the country.

It was nearly five when Burleson pulled up to the front gate. The Joneses were already in the back seat. Fannie told her children she would be back by dark, and the four of them drove off in Burleson's new Ford.

"This is quite a ride!" exclaimed Carrie.

"Indeed," added her husband, Lee. "Robert, you have bought yourself a very fine car."

The ride to the cemetery was short, but as they drove up they noticed several cars parked there.

"Let's not disturb them" said Fannie. "Can we go for a drive and then come back?" she asked Robert.

"Sure. It's a perfect day for riding and enjoying springtime," he responded as he drove down the road toward Georgetown. "After we get to Georgetown, I'll drive us out to Weir."

"Oh, yes," said Carrie. "The river and flowers will make a perfect ride."

The mood in the car was lighthearted as the four of them exchanged stories. Robert drove slowly, a little over ten m.p.h., as they reminisced about Charly. Robert also had many stories to tell. As a traveling salesman, he heard every good story that anyone told, especially the ones about traveling salesmen.

After leaving Georgetown and driving through Jonah, Fannie suggested they stop by Mrs. Barrington's. She, like Fannie, was a widow with five children to raise. They always enjoyed swapping stories.

"Well, I hate to break up such a good time, but it'll be dark soon and we need to head back to Weir," Robert said. The four of them said their goodbyes to Mrs. Barrington and headed for the car.

As they drove through Jonah, Carrie said, "Thank you, Robert. This has been a wonderful Sunday drive." Her husband and Fannie echoed the thank you. It was then Robert noticed that the car in front of him was moving very slowly.

"I thought *I* was going slow," said Robert as he passed the slower moving Ford. "They can't be going more than five miles an hour."

"Very curious," said Carrie. "Their window curtains are up, so they aren't enjoying the scenery."

Then Robert noticed a second Ford further out ahead, also creeping along. As he passed the first car and was between the two slowly moving cars, he heard the gravel fly as the car behind him accelerated and pulled even with his car.

Then the lead car came to a complete stop right in front of him. Robert hit his brakes. He didn't have time to think, but when his car came to a stop, it was trapped. A car in front. A car on one side. A ditch on the other side.

Four men immediately jumped out of the car by Robert's side. Four men, all armed with .45 pistols.

Robert asked, "What seems to be the trouble, gentlemen?"

As the driver of the car to the side screamed "Don't talk to him," the first of the armed men struck Robert with a pistol.

As two of the men grabbed Robert and pulled

41

him out of the car through the window, the other two struck him repeatedly with their pistols.

Lee and Carrie sat paralyzed with fear in the back seat. But Fannie, with her heart racing, jumped out of the passenger side and ran screaming toward the other side of the car. As she rounded the front of the car, she saw it: one of the robbers had dropped his pistol. She grabbed it and came up ready to fire. Then she felt the huge man with his strong grip.

"Nice try, little lady." He ripped the gun from her hand and pushed her to the ground.

"Get him into the back seat and let's go," said the driver.

They pushed Burleson into the back seat and shoved him half on the floor and half on the seat, face downward.

"Get that sack over his head before he sees our faces any more," said one of the men.

They took a cloth sack and pulled it over Robert's head.

"I don't know why we need to worry about him. After he's had some Klan justice, he'll be too scared to say anything." They all laughed.

This Klan outing was not like a Konklave. There was no ceremony, no ritual, no singing. Just five armed kidnappers filled with hate and one helpless victim.

The men were vulgar and profane. They soon began to taunt Robert.

"So you are going to kill twenty-one Ku Klux are you?" taunted one.

"You were warned, Burleson. You deserve everything we are going to give you," sneered another.

Robert's head throbbed from where the pistol butts had hit him. He could tell he was bleeding, but he was wedged between the seat and the floor too tightly to move. His face, covered with the sack, was pressed against the floor. He felt every bump in the road. And every one sent a shot of pain through his throbbing head.

The car came to a stop.

"Hurry!" cried the driver.

The men dragged Robert from the car and let his head hit the ground. They stood him upright and pushed him a short distance. He felt them grab and then lift him.

"Let's go," he heard.

Several of the men jumped into what he assumed was the back of the truck. He heard the engine start and the gears being shifted.

"What are you going to do?" Robert managed to gasp.

He felt the gun butt crash into the back of his head at the same time he heard the loud "Shut up!"

There were at least four men in the back of the truck with him. Their taunts grew louder, as did their profanity.

Robert lay as still as he could and kept absolutely quiet. In his present condition, he was powerless to resist four armed men. He was already feeling weak from the beating he had received.

It was only a matter of minutes before the truck came to a stop.

A chain was locked around his neck. He was pulled to a small tree where thorns or barbed wire was soon cutting into his stomach. The men tied his hands behind his back, ripped off his pants, and began to beat him with a leather strap. One man kept a gun by his head.

The men took turns flogging him with the strap. They became drunk with power as their taunts, vulgarity, and profanity became worse and worse with each blow.

"The Klan will not be defied!" screamed one.

Burleson could only endure the pain. He was totally helpless. If only it would stop. Nothing in his life had prepared him to deal with the savageness of the beating he was receiving. He couldn't even tell what the men were screaming at him. They seemed like a pack of wild animals.

"Let's don't kill him," one of the men finally called out.

They unfastened him from the tree, loaded him into the truck, and drove a short distance. Robert guessed it wasn't half a mile.

"That hackberry tree will do," said one as they pulled him from the truck.

The Klansmen carried Robert to the tree and wrapped the loose end of the chain from his neck around the tree.

"Where's the other lock?" asked one.

"It must be back in the truck," responded another.

"No time to get it." Robert felt the sack being removed from his head.

"Pour!"

He was barely able to close his eyes as the tar hit his head. The black, gooey mess was soon over his hair, eyes, mouth, and nose and dripping down to his shoulders.

"Everyone in town will see you now, Burleson. You'll never defy the Klan again."

He could hear the men laughing as they ran back to the truck and drove off.

Robert gasped for air because the tar had clogged up his mouth and nose. Slowly an airway developed and his breathing, while difficult, became steady.

He took stock of his situation. His entire body felt pain, as much pain as a man could endure. His neck was chained to the tree, but his hands and feet were free. He slowly opened his eyes and shut them again. He had been able to see but didn't want the tar to seep into his eyes.

With his hands, he tried to clear his eyes, mouth,

and nose the best he could. He then reached for the chain around his neck. It was tied securely but he followed it with his hands to the tree. He gave it a few tugs and it loosened. He tugged harder and came free of the tree.

He was on the north side of Taylor City Hall square. Across the street he saw some lights. He was weak, but he knew he needed help. As he stumbled through the dark, he kept his eyes fixed on the light. That light was his only hope. He had to make it.

Mrs. Harbor, who ran the boarding house across from Taylor City Hall, heard the banging on the door. By the time she opened the door, the man had fallen down in a heap on the front porch.

"Mercy!" she shouted. "Get help right now!"

Constable Louis Lowe received the phone call at his house as he was preparing to leave for the Sunday evening church service. He sprinted the short distance to the Harbor House.

Robert was still on the front porch when the constable arrived. Several of the boarders were standing around.

"Let me take a look," said Louis.

As the onlookers parted, Louis saw the tar-soaked, beaten body and let out a gasp.

"Quick, now," he called out. "Let's carry him across to the fire hall. Someone call Dr. Stromberg or Dr. Zorn and have them meet me over there."

Several of the men boarders helped Louis carry Robert across the street. They placed him on one of the firemen's beds.

"Get some coal oil. We can use that to get the tar off."

Just then, Dr. Zorn arrived. He looked at the patient, lying on his stomach on the bed. Robert Burleson's entire backside, from his waist to knees, had been beaten raw. The tar still covered his head wounds. For a moment, Dr. Zorn paused, stunned by

45

what he saw. Then he removed his coat, rolled up his sleeves, and began to clean and bandage the wounds.

As the doctor began his work, Louis went to the phone and placed a call to Lee Allen. He explained the situation to the sheriff. "It won't take much guesswork to figure out what group is behind this," he told the sheriff.

"Louis, I'll be right there. We have to act tonight if we want to get the evidence we need. Can the victim tell you what happened?"

"He's weak and in a lot of pain, but he was answering the doctor's questions."

"Try to get some information from him," said the sheriff. "We can start questioning witnesses as soon as I get to Taylor."

Louis went back to the bed where Burleson was being treated by two doctors now. He began to use the coal oil to remove as much tar as possible while the doctors treated the rest of his body.

Slowly and with a weak voice, Burleson was able to relate the story to Louis.

By the time Sheriff Allen and one of his deputies arrived, the doctors were ready to transport Burleson to the local hospital.

Louis had enough details to know what needed to be done. He briefed Sheriff Allen and his deputy. They made a short list of what witnesses they could talk to that night.

"We need to get some of them questioned before they have time to cook up a story," said the sheriff.

The three lawmen each went in a separate direction. "We'll meet back here about midnight," said the sheriff.

After the other two men left, Sheriff Allen went to the phone and placed a call.

"Sorry to disturb you on Easter Sunday night, Dan,

but I thought you'd want to know right away." After Allen told the story, he said, "You and I have talked about the Klan before. This time it's real, I'm going to find the witnesses. You need to be very careful."

"Don't worry —" started Dan, but the sheriff cut him off.

"I mean it. These guys are playing for keeps. Dan, this is the worst beat man I ever saw!"

5

A First Step Towards Justice

Whoosh!

The roar of the cross being ignited pierced the cool, crisp air. The flaming wooden cross, wrapped with kerosene-soaked burlap, lit up the whole of Turner's pasture. Taylor Klan No. 117 was once again conducting an initiation as twenty "aliens" were being naturalized as "citizens" of the Invisible Empire.

"Citizens of the Empire," intoned the Exalted Cyclops, John Wilkins. "Tonight, the Invisible Empire continues to grow."

There were at least two hundred white-robed members gathered in the pasture for the initiation. It was a ceremony that had occurred frequently as the Taylor Klan was thriving. The Klan staged frequent parades, held family picnics, raised money for charities, and until two days earlier, had relied on threats and intimidation rather than violence to rid the area of suspected evildoers.

The initiation ceremony continued as the Cyclops carefully followed the rituals outlined in the Kloran. Finally, the moment came for the new recruits to take their solemn oath.

Each of the twenty men placed his right hand on a Bible and repeated the oath after the Cyclops. The men promised to be loyal to the Klan and its principles, do business with fellow Klansmen, obey all Klan rules, and maintain absolute secrecy about the Klan and its members.

The Konklave concluded with the two hundred Klansmen singing the Kloxology. The flaming cross continued to burn brightly as the men made their ways to their cars.

"Olen," called the Cyclops to Olen Gossett, the chapter's Klaliff or vice president. "Could you gather the rest of the Klokann? We need to have a special meeting."

The Klokann, the five officers of the Taylor Klan, were soon gathered underneath a pecan tree on the edge of the pasture.

"Gentlemen, we need to discuss last Sunday's incident," began the Cyclops.

"All we need to do is cheer about the 'incident,'" one of the men said. "What we need to discuss is our idiot sheriff and worthless constable out questioning all these witnesses."

"Perhaps they should get the next warning," suggested another man.

"Hold on," said the Cyclops. "We aren't going to threaten the law. We all know Sheriff Allen is no friend of the Klan. But he can investigate all he wants. The Klan wasn't involved in this beating. Even if it was some of our members, they were simply acting on their own. But we do need to protect the good name of the Invisible Empire, so I'm suggesting we offer a reward for anyone who can prove that Taylor Klan 117 was involved."

Laughter broke out among the men.

"Great idea," said the Klabee. "Let's make it $500 and give a copy of the reward notice to the newspapers."

"But what if Allen pins some charges against one of our members?" asked one of them.

"The Klan is above the law," said the Cyclops. "Have you ever heard of a Klansman being convicted of anything?"

The men laughed again.

They set about writing the reward notice and making arrangements to get it to the newspapers.

As they were finishing, the Cyclops turned to Olen Gossett, the Klaliff. "Olen, you are being unusually quiet tonight. Is anything wrong?"

"I'm worried about the sheriff's investigation. He and Louis Lowe have talked to darn near everyone in Taylor. Eventually, they'll get some testimony."

"Olen, I don't know who did the beating, and I don't want to know," said the Cyclops. "But no Klansman will ever talk to the law about another Klansman. And remember, no Klansman has ever been convicted. Not here, not anywhere in Texas, not anywhere in the country. It's never going to happen."

That morning, the Monday after Easter, Dan Moody took an early morning train from Austin. He traveled a hundred miles east to the small town of Sealy, the seat of Austin County. Dan had been asked to be a special prosecutor for a series of trials involving a gun and knife battle in the middle of a local street. While his mind was back in Williamson County with Sheriff Allen, he had to spend two weeks in Sealy trying the cases.

Dan talked with Sheriff Lee Allen every night from his hotel room. Dan followed the investigation in the *Austin American*, which arrived in Sealy every afternoon on the train.

On Thursday afternoon, with his local trial concluded for the day, Dan was sitting in his hotel room when Sheriff Allen called. On Dan's bed lay the last four issues of the *Austin American*. Monday's front page headlines told the story.

TAYLOR MAN IS FLOGGED — VICTIM'S CONDITION SERIOUS

Tuesday's and Wednesday's gave more details.

CHAIN SAWED FROM NECK

WHIP INQUIRY IN COURT TODAY

Thursday's paper was the biggest. A banner headline stretched across the entire front page.

FIVE TAYLOR MEN ARRESTED AFTER INVESTIGATION OF SALESMAN FLOGGING — CITY MARSHALL IS CHARGED.

"I see you got your arrests," Dan said.

Lee sounded proud. "Those were the four in the car that jumped out with their pistols. The fifth was Chief Hewlitt. He was the driver."

"How does our evidence look?"

"Things happened fast, but Fannie Campbell told me she got a good look at the gunmen and she can identify them. The Joneses stayed in the back seat and may not be much help with the identification. But Carrie Jones got enough of a look at the driver to describe Bob Hewlitt pretty good."

"How's Burleson?"

"He looks terrible. He's weak and in pain, but he'll live. Probably be well enough to go home in a few more days. It will be a long time before he's good for anything other than lying around the house."

"Can he help make an identification in court?"

"I'm not exactly sure, because he hasn't seen any of them. He gave us some pretty good descriptions, but we won't know for sure until he sees them. He did give us a pretty good description of the truck he was transferred into. It was an Overland."

"Well, keep working on the witnesses, Lee. Those ole boys had to be somewhere before the crime and after the crime. There are plenty of people who have information that will be helpful."

"We're thinking alike. Louis Lowe is working Taylor pretty good. He's got a lead on Murray Jackson borrowing a pistol a few hours before the beating and then returning it later that evening."

"Sounds good. Anything else?"

"Well, it's not been easy. Some of the witnesses claim not to have any memory and some seem to be flat out lying. We *are* dealing with the Klan, you know."

"How's the general public reacting?"

"They are pretty much disgusted that this could happen in Williamson County. But, of course, the pro-Klan folks insist the Klan wasn't responsible. The Taylor Klan even put up a $500 reward for anyone that can prove the Klan was involved."

"It would take a pretty good imagination not to believe this was the Klan's work," Dan said.

"Oh, people believe what they want to believe. As far as the Klan goes, some people will never believe anything bad about them."

"Perhaps this time they went too far."

There was a silence on the phone as the two men thought about the prospects of a long, complicated prosecution.

"Well, keep up the good work, Lee. I'll get to Georgetown as soon as these trials are over. I'd like to take Burleson to the grand jury the first part of May."

The Williamson County courthouse was a massive three story structure of light-brown brick that stood in the middle of the Georgetown square. On each of its four sides, broad steps led up to the first floor entrance. Above each entrance stretched a wide second-story porch. From each porch, four huge concrete columns rose to the top of the third floor. Above the third floor was a two-story copper dome. A clock face was imbedded on each side of the dome; a huge bell rang out each hour. A statue of Lady Justice topped the dome, complete with a scale in one hand and a sword in the other.

The courthouse, built twelve years earlier, was the showplace of a prosperous, growing county. Inside, marble wainscoting lined all the walls, polished wood accented all the doorways, and an airy rotunda opened a cathedral-like vault underneath the top of the dome, high above.

The grand jury room, along with the jury dormitory, was located on the third floor. The courtroom and the county attorney's office were located on the second floor. There was no separate office for the district attorney — his main office was in the Travis County courthouse — but Dan Moody made himself at home in the county attorney's office whenever he was in Georgetown.

Normally, Dan would meet with the grand jury one day each month. They would hear evidence on a few routine cases and vote to bring formal criminal charges, called an indictment. Then the grand jurors would return to their homes and their work until the next month.

This grand jury session was different. Dan was in the process of presenting evidence of a single crime, the Burleson flogging. He was calling more than a hundred witnesses before the grand jury. To help, he had recruited a team of six other lawyers, including County Attorney Albert Evans, former County Attorney Harry Graves, and former County Judge Richard Critz. Graves and Critz were both well thought of, popular lawyers who were about fifteen years older than Dan. While Dan wanted them on his trial team and valued their expertise, he was the district attorney, and he intended to do most of the work himself, especially the courtroom work. The other six lawyers interviewed witnesses and worked with Sheriff Allen and his deputies to get all the witnesses to the courthouse. Dan, however, did nearly all the questioning of witnesses in the grand jury room.

The first day of grand jury testimony went well. Burleson and Mrs. Campbell testified. The suspects, along with several other men, were brought into the grand jury room. Mrs. Campbell positively identified Murray Jackson, Olen Gossett, and Dewey Ball. She wasn't quite as certain about Sam Threadgill, and she had not seen Chief Bob Hewlitt. Burleson, who had not made any official identifications, tentatively identified Jackson, Gossett, and Ball also. He was not sure about the other two.

Dan had two positive eyewitnesses on three defendants. He expected the grand jury to indict at least those three. Next, he could concentrate on identifying the other two suspects and strengthening his case against Jackson, Gossett, and Ball.

Dan began the second day by calling Rev. A. A. Davis and K. C. Baker. It was too bad that Mrs. Campbell had burned the warning note from the Klan that Davis had delivered. Could Dan hope to get Davis and Baker to admit what they had done? Laughing in response, Sheriff Lee Allen warned Dan that Davis and Baker would not cooperate. But grand juries met in secret, and Dan was hoping Davis and Baker might be more cooperative if they didn't have to worry about a fellow Klansman hearing their testimony.

The grand jury room was just big enough for a large table and fourteen chairs. Dan sat at one end, next to the grand jury foreman. The witnesses sat at the far end. Between them, the twelve grand jurors sat, six at a side, along the length of the table.

After everyone was seated, Dan briefly outlined his plan for the day and then asked the bailiff to bring Reverend Davis into the room.

As Davis walked in, the bailiff shut the door and

stood guard outside in the hall. Dan rose, motioned for Davis to go to the far end of the table, and then greeted him professionally.

"Before we begin, Reverend Davis, I need to give you an oath," said Dan.

Davis nodded and began listening to the oath as Dan gave it. Dan, as most district attorneys, knew the oath by heart but to impress witnesses, he had it burned into a piece of leather and tacked to a small board. He always held it up as he swore the witness in. The first part of the oath required the witnesses to keep secret everything that happened before the grand jury. It concluded, "And that you will true answers make to such questions as may be propounded to you by the grand jury or under its direction, so help you God."

"I do," Davis said solemnly.

"Have a seat, Mr. Davis." Dan planned on being in control, so he dropped the Reverend title.

Davis had barely sat down when he blurted, "You aren't going to put anything over on me."

"Excuse me, Mr. Davis, if you simply tell us the truth, as you a moment ago swore to do, then you'll have nothing to worry about."

Davis was taken back by Dan's calm but confident demeanor. Dan ran through some preliminary questions then got to the heart of the matter.

"Mr. Davis, have you ever been to Weir, Texas?"

"No, sir."

"Have you ever had a conversation with a barber named K. C. Baker about a salesman named Burleson?"

"No, I have not."

"Did you go to Weir, Texas, earlier this year and deliver a notice to R. W. Burleson from the Georgetown Ku Klux Klan?"

"No, I did not."

"Have you ever had a conversation with a man named Burleson?"

"I'm not sure his name, but a man who could be this Burleson came up to me in the street in Georgetown, talking foolish about some notice from the Klan. But I told him I knew nothing about it."

"So you absolutely deny any connection with Weir, with Baker, or with delivering this Klan notice?"

"I deny it. I'm not your man. You got the wrong man," Davis insisted.

Dan asked a few more questions and got nowhere.

"I'll give you one more chance to tell us about the note you delivered in Weir."

The grand jury room became silent. Davis looked directly into Dan's eyes. "You have the wrong man."

Dan excused the witness and then called K. C. Baker. He didn't want Baker and Davis to communicate. Baker had to be worried that Davis had told the truth.

Baker entered the grand jury room a moment after Davis had left. Dan swore him in, began with some preliminary questions, and then asked, "Do you know Reverend A. A. Davis?"

"Not really. I've heard talk around town that he was supposed to be a Klan preacher who served a notice in Weir, but I've never met the man. I guess he was the fellow that testified just before me?"

"You guessed correctly. Do you know the man who just left?"

"No, just know of him, like I explained."

"Are you a member of the Ku Klux Klan?" asked Dan.

"No, I'm not."

"Did you ever report about R. W. Burleson to the Klan?"

"No."

"Did you give directions to anyone as to where Mrs. Campbell lived, so they could deliver a notice to Burleson or Mrs. Campbell?"

"No, Mr. Moody. I've heard a lot of talk about this. It's not true. I didn't do anything. I don't know anything. I wasn't involved."

Dan continued his questions but got nowhere. Davis and Baker were sticking with their stories. Dan wasn't going to get any help with his case from them.

The grand jury got to hear several more witnesses before they broke for lunch. Dan headed straight for the county attorney's office. Inside, the other attorneys and Sheriff Allen waited. While grand jury proceedings were secret, Dan was allowed to discuss them with other prosecutors and the officers conducting the investigation.

Dan brought the group up to date. They discussed strategy for the afternoon. Dan listened to various suggestions, then he turned to Sheriff Allen.

"Lee, we need to take a chance if we are going to get any more of these men identified. Of the three we have now — Jackson, Gossett, and Ball — who do you think is the weakest?"

"Definitely, Murray Jackson," said Lee. "But you grew up with them, they were all three born and raised in Taylor."

"Jackson's my guess too," said Dan. "He never has amounted to much of anything. He doesn't even have a job, except helping at his father's business on and off."

Dan outlined his plan to call Jackson, along with three others, G. S. Dunbar, Godfrey Lottus, and W. E. Posey. Those three were, according to the best information Louis Lowe could come up with, Klansmen from Elgin, a few miles south of Taylor. They likely were the men in the other car who had not been seen by Burleson, but who later helped flog him.

"What do you think, Lee?" asked Dan.

"It's worth a try. We have several options if they won't talk."

"I say we march them right down to the courtroom and have Judge Hamilton order them to talk. If they don't, the judge can give them immunity, and if they still refuse, he can hold them in contempt of court and send them to jail."

"And if they *do* talk?" asked the sheriff.

"Well, with immunity, they're home free, of course, but we can still use them as witnesses against Ball and Gossett."

"I don't want to let anyone get away with this," said Allen.

"But we need to have the strongest possible case," explained Dan.

The sheriff and the other lawyers saw the advantages of Dan's plan. They prepared for the afternoon session.

The afternoon grand jury session began with Murray Jackson called as the first witness. Dan swore him in and reminded him that he had been arrested for the crime which the grand jury was looking into.

"So I don't have to talk to the grand jury and I won't," Jackson said in a voice barely audible.

"Murray, relax," responded Dan. "You and I have known each other for a long time. You need to consider —"

"No. My lawyer warned me about what you would try to do. I'm not going to talk."

Dan continued to try to engage Jackson in a conversation about childhood days in Taylor. But Jackson, while clearly nervous and talking very softly, refused to answer any questions.

"Very well." Dan spoke with an air of resignation. "Listen carefully to these questions, Murray. Did you see a man named R. W. Burleson on Easter Sunday?"

"I refuse to answer."

"Did you have a pistol in your hand on Easter Sunday?"

"I'm not talking."

"Did you hit R. W. Burleson on the head with the pistol?"

"Not answering."

"Who were the other men with you?"

"Not answering."

"Did you flog R.W. Burleson with a strap on Easter Sunday?"

"Not answering."

"Did you take R.W. Burleson to the Taylor City Hall, chain him to a tree, and pour tar on him?"

"Not answering." He was clearly uncomfortable and nervous, but he was not going to give in.

"Last chance, Murray. Let's make this easier."

"No."

"Okay, we'll get the bailiff." At the door, Dan called into the hall.

The bailiff came into the room and escorted Murray Jackson, Dan Moody, and all twelve grand jurors to the second floor, where Judge Hamilton held court. It was a public courtroom, so there were a couple dozen people there, sitting alone and reading, or whispering in twos and threes. The judge was at his bench, bent over paperwork.

D. L. Noble, the grand jury foreman, took a seat in the front row of the courtroom. The other grand jurors filed in alongside him. Dan, the bailiff, and Jackson stood to the side.

Judge James Hamilton looked up. "Mr. Foreman, does the grand jury have a question?" A district attorney for a decade and a judge for almost that long, Judge Hamilton knew what the grand jury wanted before the foreman responded.

"Sort of. We have a witness who has refused to answer our questions."

The judge looked first at Jackson and then turned to Dan. "Is that correct, Mr. District Attorney?"

"Yes, sir. Murray Jackson has refused to answer the following questions." Dan recited the questions for Judge Hamilton.

"Is that correct, Mr. Jackson?"

"Yes, sir."

"Excuse me, your honor. A. E. Wood representing the witness, Mr. Jackson."

There was an immediate hush in the courtroom. Senator A.E. Wood did not need an introduction. He was well known to everyone in the county as an able lawyer and the senator who represented them in the state legislature. Dan's heart skipped a beat. Senator Wood knew everyone and everything in the county. The Klan had hired Wood, the most powerful lawyer in the county. But Dan had dealt with the best lawyers in the county before.

"Yes, Senator, do you wish to be heard?" asked Judge Hamilton.

"I object to this proceeding," the senator stated forcefully. "My client has already been arrested, falsely arrested I might add, and the district attorney has no business hauling him in front of the grand jury. He has a right not to testify against himself."

"Yes, Senator, but the grand jury has the right to question him, and if he refuses to answer, the court can grant him immunity," responded Judge Hamilton. "I presume that was going to be the district attorney's next request?"

"That's correct, your honor," said Dan.

"Very well. Mr. Jackson, the state has requested immunity for you. I am going to grant that request and order you to answer the grand jury's questions.

Any answers you give which incriminate you, cannot be used against you in any later trial. Senator Wood, I'm sure, can explain this to you."

The grand jury and Dan then returned to their third-floor room. Jackson talked briefly with Senator Wood, and then he too went back to the grand jury room. No one else was allowed into the grand jury room, so Senator Wood sat outside in the hallway. The proceedings didn't take long, because Jackson still refused to answer the questions.

Once again the grand jurors, Dan, Jackson, the bailiff, and now Senator Wood, along with several other witnesses marched back into Judge Hamilton's courtroom. This time, it was more crowded as the word had spread throughout the courthouse and around the square.

Judge Hamilton looked up from his bench with a very stern look. "Mr. Moody, you are back?"

"Yes, sir, despite the court's grant of immunity, the witness refuses to answer the questions."

"Mr. Jackson, do you refuse to answer the grand jury's questions?"

Jackson looked at Senator Wood. The senator nodded.

"Yes, sir," said Jackson to the judge.

"Then I have no choice but to find you in contempt of this court. I hereby order the sheriff to take you into custody until such time as you are willing to answer these questions. I also fine you $100."

"Judge, note my objection to these proceedings. We intend to file an immediate appeal," said Senator Wood.

The word "we" surprised Dan. He turned his head and saw that Senator Wood had been joined by three other lawyers. The Klan had hired a whole team.

One of Sheriff Allen's deputies soon appeared in

court to lead Jackson to jail. Meanwhile, Dan returned to the grand jury room. He called the three Elgin Klansmen—Dunbar, Loftus, and Posey.

One by one, they went through the steps again. As with Murray Jackson, they refused to answer the questions, they were given immunity, and they refused again. Judge Hamilton found all three in contempt of court. He sentenced them to pay fines of $100, same as Jackson, and ordered them to jail until they answered the questions, same as Jackson.

After the last of them was led off by the deputy, Dan returned to the grand jury and called a series of cooperative witnesses until the early evening. Most of the witnesses took only a few minutes to relate some detail of the events on Easter Sunday.

Finally, after two days of hard work, Dan finished with the last of his more than one hundred witnesses. It was now time for him to sum up the evidence.

Dan explained the charges to the grand jury. Assault with a prohibited weapon. He read it from the book. Then he said it all again in less technical language.

Taking the events in the order they happened on Easter Sunday, Dan then listed and explained his evidence. He summarized it defendant by defendant: strong against Jackson, Ball, and Gossett; flimsy against Threadgill and Hewlitt. Dan told them how frustrated he was that they hadn't been able to identify the other participants, but expressed hope that perhaps one of the jailed men would change his mind and answer their questions.

Dan concluded, "Gentlemen, each of us knows the Klan reign of terror has gone on for over two years now. They threaten, intimidate, flog, tar, and feather. And they even kill. They are as un-American a group of lawless cowards as has ever walked on American soil. And they have never been convicted

62

of a crime, never been held accountable for their law-lessness. The first step towards breaking the Klan will be to obtain a conviction in court. But we can only do this if you return indictments. Consider the evidence, gentlemen, and return indictments against these criminals for their actions."

With that, Dan departed. He was not allowed to remain while the grand jurors discussed the case and voted on whether to indict.

Dan walked downstairs to the county attorney's office. Sheriff Allen and the attorneys had already gathered in the office.

Dan thanked them all for their hard work. "And Sheriff, you and Louis did a fantastic job. I think we have as strong a case as could be put together."

"Now, if we don't have too many Klansmen on the grand jury, we ought to get an indictment," commented one of the prosecutors. They all laughed.

"Let's don't worry too much about that. It takes only nine of twelve votes for an indictment," said Dan. "Surely, we can count on at least nine following the law."

Unfortunately, Dan thought, at trial he would need a unanimous verdict. All twelve trial jurors would have to vote guilty. The men's conversation drifted to the weather and politics.

But it was only a few more minutes before the bailiff appeared. "They are ready, Mr. Moody. They are coming down to the courtroom."

The lawyers and sheriff walked across the rotunda to the courtroom. The grand jurors were already seat-ed in the jury box. The courtroom held several dozen spectators, some of whom had been witnesses, along with several newspaper reporters and, of course, Senator Wood with his team of lawyers.

Judge Hamilton's bailiff called the court to order.

"Do you have a report, Mr. Foreman?" the judge asked.

"Yes, sir." The foreman stood as he responded.

"Very well, what is it?"

"The grand jury returns three indictments, charging Murray Jackson, Dewey Ball, and Olen Gossett with the felony of aggravated assault with a prohibited weapon."

There seemed to be a collective gasp in the courtroom. It then became very quiet. Indictments, especially when backed up with two eyewitnesses, were routine. But everyone seemed to grasp the importance of these cases. The indictments were against Jackson, Ball, and Gossett, but everyone knew that this was a case against the Ku Klux Klan.

6

Three Months
to Trial

"Well, they're out. I hated to open the jail cell door," Sheriff Lee Allen explained as he walked into the county attorney's office where Dan was sitting.

Dan and his team of lawyers had spent the last month fighting numerous appeals filed by Senator Wood. All the appeals asked that the Klansmen be released. But Judge Hamilton had the right to put them in jail for contempt, and Dan fought hard to make sure they stayed put. None of the suspects gave in, and all four refused to answer the questions. Today, however, was the last day of the grand jury's term, and the contempt order expired with the grand jury.

"Well, thirty-five days in jail and a hundred dollar fine is more than any Klansman has served before," said Dan.

"Let's hope it's the first installment of a lot longer prison sentence," said Lee. "What's next?"

"We still need to follow up on some of those leads Louis came up with. If we can prove that Murray Jackson borrowed a pistol Easter Sunday and then returned it after the beating, that would be a solid piece of evidence to back up the eyewitnesses."

"Louis is still working on it. He's also trying to

find witnesses linking Jackson to the Overland truck Burleson described."

"Well, both of you need to keep working. We need to try our strongest case first. The case against Jackson looks like it will be our best, especially if we can tie him to the pistol and the truck."

"I guess you heard about the new defense team addition, W. W. Hair," said Lee.

"No, I hadn't. But I figured as much," said Dan.

W. W. Hair, of nearby Temple, was the best criminal lawyer in central Texas, maybe the whole state. Although he seldom came to Georgetown, he had a reputation for getting his clients off.

"That really makes sense. They have the most powerful, influential lawyer in Senator Wood, and now the best trial lawyer in these parts," said Dan. "I guess I don't have to wonder where the money is coming from."

"The best I can tell is each Klansman has kicked in fifteen dollars, some a lot more. My guess is they have raised ten thousand. Maybe even two or three times that. By the way, do you think you can get this case to trial by the July date the judge set?"

"Senator Wood is pushing for a later date. I can probably get him to agree to September. Maybe it won't be quite so hot by then."

"Okay, Dan. Louis and I will keep working on witnesses for you. But now we need to have a serious sheriff-to-D.A. talk. You quit being a lawyer and listen."

Dan knew when Lee was serious, and this was one of those times.

"Clayton Peeler."

Dan started to say something.

"No. You sit and listen." Lee set his mouth and glared until Dan settled back in his chair. "Clayton Peeler is a name you need to remember."

Clayton Peeler had been killed in Austin by some unknown Klansmen back in December 1921. No one was sure whether Peeler had been in the wrong place at the wrong time or was part of an anti-Klan group, but the story had dominated the Austin newspaper for six months. Peeler had been shot to death in an alley in downtown Austin. The alley happened to be behind the Klan meeting hall on San Jacinto Street.

The Klan had been meeting that night, and some anti-Klan men had been sitting outside, taking down the names of everyone who entered the hall. Some Klansmen had come outside and threatened them, which caused them to leave. A few minutes later, Clayton Peeler was driving his Dodge automobile down the alley. The Klansmen assumed he was part of the anti-Klan group and opened fire on his car, killing Peeler instantly.

Dan's predecessor as district attorney, Ben Robertson, launched an all-out grand jury investigation but was unable to develop enough evidence for an indictment. Both the Austin police chief and the Travis County sheriff refused to answer questions and were held in contempt of court. Only after several months of delaying their jail sentences did they reluctantly answer the grand jury's questions, too little too late.

"Dan, the men who killed Peeler got away with murder. They know it, every Klansman knows it, and everyone else knows it too. You need to be careful. Don't take any chances. The Klan plays for keeps."

"Your advice is well taken," Dan told his friend. "I'll be careful."

The Texas summer was in full force by mid-July. Temperatures were in the high 90s every day; soon, they would hit the 100s. One afternoon, Dan was working in his office in the Travis County court-

67

house, which was located on Congress Avenue directly across from the south entrance of the state capitol. He had removed his coat and rolled up his sleeves first thing in the morning, and the ceiling fan was churning. Still, it was too hot an afternoon to be working. Dan welcomed his secretary's announcement that his friend and former law partner, Harris Melasky, had dropped by to see him.

"Harris! Great to see you. I needed a break." Dan cheerfully shook Melasky's hand.

"We have both been working hard," noted Harris. "Your successes have all been in the newspapers. Everyone in Taylor talks about you."

"I'm not sure it's good talk."

Harris smiled. "Mostly good. It does seem the town is divided over one of your cases."

"Texas and the nation are divided over the Klan, Harris. There's no reason for Taylor to be any different."

"Well, that's really why I came to see you. I know you are working hard, and I thought you might need an old friend to talk to."

"Harris, I'm going to prosecute the case. A district attorney must stand for the law and a proper system of justice, not mob rule."

"You are going to destroy your career, a very promising career. The Klan is too big and too powerful. You have already made your point. You locked the Klansmen up for a month. There won't be any more Klan violence in Williamson County."

"I have to do more than make a point. I mean to stop the violence, to break the Klan, and the best way to do that is to get a criminal conviction."

"You won't get a conviction. You won't. They've committed hundreds of crimes all over Texas, all over the country. Not one single conviction. They've hired two of the best lawyers around. They have plenty of good citizens ready to testify for them. And besides, how are you going to keep a Klansman off the jury? It's not like they will admit to their membership."

"I don't know how I'm going to do it. I do know I've got to try."

"Dan, you can't do it. It's impossible. Now quit while you're ahead. See if Hair and Wood won't have their clients plead guilty for a fine and a few days in jail. You'll still have made your point, and you'll save your career."

"That would be a career not worth saving," said Dan.

The two men sat in silence. Finally, Harris spoke.

"They control every elected office in Houston, every elected office in Dallas. They elected our last United States senator, there are millions of them nationwide. The district attorney in Dallas stood up to them, and he got clobbered in the last election. And let's not forget the sheriff in Waco—he was nearly indicted for trying to stop the Klan. All of that, and Dan Moody is going to throw his career away over principle."

Dan returned his friend's even gaze.

"Well, no one has ever talked you out of anything, Dan. And to be honest, I didn't think I could either."

Harris reached into his coat pocket and pulled out an envelope. "Most everyone is betting against you, but this will finance your other lawyers. You will need them to keep up with Senator Wood and his pals." Harris handed Dan the envelope filled with cash.

"And who gave the money?"

"Don't worry, Dan. It's all legitimate. Some former district attorneys, business people in the Liberty League — some of it's from Austin, some from Taylor, some from Georgetown."

Finally, Dan smiled. "Turns out quite a lot of people believe in our country and our system of justice."

"Hmmm," said Harris, nodding. "Turns out."

Dan looked down at the calendar in front of him. September 16, 1923. He could scarcely believe that the trial was scheduled to begin tomorrow. Four months of preparation, and they could finally begin.

Dan, Sheriff Allen, Louis Lowe, the constable, and the five lawyers who were helping had spent all Sunday afternoon in the county attorney's office going over the evidence.

The men reviewed the statements of more than a hundred witnesses. Dan carefully pruned the list. He selected ten witnesses that he would call to prove Murray Jackson's guilt. But he had also reviewed the statements of some fifty other witnesses whom they thought the defense might call. Dan wanted to be prepared for anything the defense raised. Dan had a near photographic memory, and he wanted each witness and their statements etched into his mind.

It was normal for the prosecution to be worried about its case the night before trial. But the men around Dan looked particularly glum.

Dan decided to broach the subject. "Either everyone is very tired or we have already been beat. What's wrong?"

The lawyers looked embarrassed, but finally Richard Critz spoke up. Judge Critz, along with Harry Graves, was older and more experienced than the other lawyers. Critz had been the county judge who ramrodded the construction of the new courthouse thirteen years earlier.

"I think we have all heard — too many times — that no one can convict the Klan. Everyone I have talked to this week, those for the Klan and those against it, seems convinced that we can't win. I mean, Dan, even my wife, who generally stays out of my cases, says it's hopeless."

"All right. I hear the same talk you hear, Judge.

70

But let's not beat ourselves. We have a solid case. Two eyewitnesses and a horrible beating."

"But how do we keep a Klansman or a sympathizer off the jury — a ringer who would never vote to convict," interrupted Albert Evans.

"Sheriff, you and Louis have been over the list of potential jurors?" asked Dan.

"Sure. We know a fair number of them, and we have checked with other people who know the ones we don't," replied the sheriff.

"And how does it look?"

"There are some who we know or are pretty sure that they belong to the Klan, and there are some that are pretty solidly against the Klan. Our real problem is there are some we don't know about. They could be in the Klan or not," said Allen.

"And they'll lie so they can get on the jury," added Evans.

"That's my job," said Dan. "I'll look them in the eye, ask them directly, and make up my mind if they are lying."

"That assumes Judge Hamilton even lets you ask about the Klan. You know the defense will object every time you bring it up," said Judge Critz.

"We also need to worry about a surprise witness," said Louis Lowe. "I keep hearing around town whispers about some surprise Hair and Wood have in store for us."

"Enough!" exclaimed Dan. "Everyone is too tired to think straight. We have a good, solid case, and we will have to rely on the good citizens of Williamson County to see that justice is done. Everyone go home and be back here at 7:30 in the morning. Good night."

Dan needed to be alone. Everything the other men said was true. How was he going to keep a ringer off the jury? Wood and Hair must have a surprise witness. Even Judge Hamilton might not let him ask about Klan membership during jury selection.

Dan tried to convince himself that this was no different from the other cases he had tried. There were always unexpected things happening, and he almost always figured a way around them.

But this case was different, and Dan knew it. The Klan had millions of members nationwide. It was a secret society, and Dan had no way of knowing who or how many members they had. He couldn't even be sure about his friends and neighbors.

Dan looked out the window at the dark night. He took a deep breath. Daniel Moody, the boy who had watched trials, was now Dan Moody, district attorney. Tomorrow, the boy would have to show he was a man, he would stand up in court and announce "The State's ready, your honor," and he would have to mean it.

7

"The State's Ready"

"All rise!" the bailiff called out as the judge walked into the courtroom from a door to the right of his bench.

The crowd quieted and rose as one. The lawyers, all seven for the state, stood around the table closest to the jury box. The six defense lawyers and Murray Jackson stood around the other table.

"The 26th Judicial District Court for the State of Texas is now in session. The Honorable James R. Hamilton, presiding," the bailiff concluded.

Judge Hamilton surveyed the courtroom and ordered everyone to be seated. All spectator seats, downstairs and in the balcony, had been taken shortly after the courthouse opened. The doors from the main hallway and the outside balcony were also open, and more spectators stood around each doorway as far as hearing distance would allow.

"Good afternoon," Judge Hamilton began. "I'm pleased to see the rain has stopped and perhaps we won't have to be building arks this September."

The courtroom erupted in laughter. On Monday, the area had been hit by a two-inch downpour. Any rain in September made everyone nervous. Two years earlier, a hurricane in the Gulf of Mexico stalled and caused a deluge which created severe flooding.

The small community of Thrall, near Taylor, had recorded a national record thirty-eight inches of rain while the rest of Williamson County had a mere twenty or so inches. So to control his courtroom, Judge Hamilton was going to be strict when he needed to be and lighthearted when he could.

"I want to remind everyone that this is a court of law. I know many of you in the audience have strong feelings about this case on trial, but there will be no outbursts. I'll call for announcements. Mr. Moody?"

Dan rose. "The State's ready, your honor."

"Mr. Hair?"

Hair rose. "The defense is ready, your honor."

"Very well, bailiff, bring the jury in."

It was Wednesday afternoon. Two and a half days of preliminaries had set the stage for the jury to now hear the first testimony in the case. Monday, the defense took up the entire day with delaying motions. First, they tried to get Judge Hamilton to completely throw out the charges and when that failed, they called fifty witnesses to testify that a change of venue should be granted to move the trial to another county. Judge Hamilton also denied that motion.

All day Tuesday was taken up with the actual jury selection. Both sides questioned fifty-two male citizens to select the twelve who were now filing into the jury box. Dan won a key victory early when Judge Hamilton allowed him to question them about membership in the Ku Klux Klan. Every one of the twelve swore that he was not a member of the Ku Klux Klan; Dan hoped they were telling the truth.

After still more legal arguments Wednesday morning, at last the testimony could begin.

"The defendant will please rise," instructed the judge. "Mr. Moody, proceed."

Dan walked to the judge's bench where the judge

handed him the pink copy of the indictment. Dan turned to look at the jury as he began to read. "In the name and by the authority of the State of Texas . . ." he boomed.

Dan stood six-feet one. He had red hair and a voice which filled the courtroom. The long months of preparation, the wrangling over technical issues with the defense were over. He now had a defendant in front of a jury. He knew that within a few minutes he would have control of the courtroom. He was prepared, the facts of his case were compelling, and the dark secrets of the Ku Klux Klan were about to be exposed to the bright sunlight of justice.

The indictment Dan read set out the charge of assault with a prohibited weapon. It detailed that on April 1, 1923, Murray Jackson assaulted R. W. Burleson by striking him on the head with a pistol. Dan concluded, reading, "Against the peace and dignity of the State. Signed by D. L. Noble, foreman of the grand jury."

"How does the defendant plead?" asked the judge.

"Not guilty," Murray Jackson spoke softly.

"Be seated. You may call your first witness, Mr. Moody," instructed the judge.

"State calls R. W. Burleson," said Dan. A murmur went through the crowd. Instead of calling the victim last, Dan was calling him first. He intended to catch the defense attorneys off guard and also convince the jury of the defendant's guilt right away.

Burleson took the oath to tell the truth and was seated.

"Will you state your name?" Dan asked.

"R. W. Burleson."

"How are you employed?"

"I'm a salesman. I sell socks for the Real Silk Hosiery Mill of Indianapolis, Indiana."

Dan inquired about Burleson's upbringing and family. He brought out Burleson's army service during World War I. Despite the defense's objection, he testified he was a relative of Albert Sidney Burleson, a well known Texas politician who was postmaster of the United States under President Woodrow Wilson.

Dan brought out testimony of the Klan warning and had Burleson recount the events of Easter Sunday. The courtroom was absolutely quiet as Burleson described the two cars, how they stopped his vehicle, and how the four men with pistols jumped out, beat him over the head, and pulled him from the car.

"Mr. Burleson, do you see the first man out of the car, the first man who struck you on the head with a pistol, the man who, with the others, pulled you from your car and continued to beat you with pistols as you lay on the ground, do you see that man in the courtroom?"

"Yes, sir."

"Would you point him out to us, please?"

Burleson looked over to the defense table and looked at Jackson. Four hundred pairs of eyes were absolutely transfixed on Burleson as he raised his right hand and pointed directly at Jackson. "That's the man."

There was a collective exhale by the entire audience followed by the beginnings of some low whispers. Judge Hamilton reached for his gavel and brought quiet back to the room.

"After you were being beaten on the ground, did any of the men grab you?" Dan resumed.

Burleson recounted how he was forced into the car, had a sack placed over his head, and was driven off into the night.

"Did any of the men say anything to you as you were being driven away?"

"Objection!" Hair jumped to his feet. "Your Honor, we are here for a trial about an assault with a pistol. Nothing more. Any other testimony about events afterward is irrelevant and should not be allowed."

"The jury is entitled to hear the entire transaction, Judge," Dan countered. "They have a right to know everything that this defendant and his co-conspirators said and did in connection with this crime."

"Your objection is overruled, Mr. Hair. Mr. Moody, you may continue."

"Well, then we will further object if the answer to this question has anything to do with a secret society. This secret society has nothing to do with the case either," Hair stated.

"If it wasn't for the Klan, there would be no crime," said Dan. "This case has everything to do with the Ku Klux Klan." Dan laid special emphasis on the final three words.

Outraged, Hair gasped. "Your Honor. I object!"

"Gentlemen, I've already ruled on the Klan issue in this case. Mr. Moody, you may question the witnesses about the facts, about what was said and done. If the Klan — or any other group — is mentioned, then so be it. Proceed, Mr. Moody."

"I'll repeat my question. Did any of the men say anything to you as you were being driven off?"

Burleson waited to get a nod from Dan before he answered. "One of them asked me if I ever threatened to kill the first twenty-one Ku Kluxes I met."

"Was that the only mention of the Klan?"

"No, it was repeated over and over. They asked about the warning I got in Weir, why I didn't obey the Klan warning."

Dan had Burleson recount the chain being put around his neck and the details of the flogging. Burleson described how his skin was ripped apart by

77

the lashes, how the Klansmen taunted him as they continued the blows. He told the jury about being loaded into the Overland truck, being driven to Taylor City Hall, being chained to the tree, and the tar being poured on his head.

Dan asked the bailiff to retrieve the chain from outside the courtroom.

"Mr. Burleson, I want to show you this chain." The heavy chain made a loud clanking as Dan took it from the bailiff, dragged it across the wooden floor, and hauled it up onto the wood rail in front of the witness. The jurors, sitting barely six feet from the witness, looked at it closely.

"That's the chain, Mr. Moody. You can see here where it was sawed from around my neck, and that black stuff on it is the tar that they poured on me."

Dan was sure that Burleson's testimony was believable, but he knew that juries like concrete evidence that they can see and touch. A heavy chain complete with hacksaw marks and tar was the perfect exhibit for this case. No matter how many legal objections the defense made or how they tried to confuse the issues, the jury would remember that chain.

Burleson testified the entire afternoon. His story was detailed and graphic. He spoke confidently, without bitterness. When he recounted the actual beating, he spoke slowly as he seemed to recall the pain. Everyone could imagine the scars he still carried. Dan sensed that the jurors and spectators, while they may have read newspaper stories or talked about the case with friends, were surprised by the severity, the savageness, and the duration of the beating.

"Pass the witness," Dan said as he finished.

"Gentlemen, it's late in the day," said Judge Hamilton. "I think everyone is exhausted. We will resume court at 8:30 tomorrow morning."

The jury began to file out. Their home for the duration of the trial was the courthouse. There was a dormitory, complete with bunkbeds, located on the third floor where they would stay.

As they walked out, Dan watched them for any sign of how they were reacting. As usual with jurors, he saw none.

Dan could imagine what was ahead. The defense attorneys were going to be vigorous, and Burleson was in for a tough cross-examination. The surprise witness they were harboring could be devastating, and the Klan's legendary power could affect witnesses. At least one Klansman, or someone who strongly supported them, could very well be on the jury. The trial had just begun.

8

"A Darkness on America"

"Mr. Burleson, I'm W. W. Hair. I'm a lawyer who practices law up the road in Temple, Texas."

Dan took a deep breath. The more polite the introduction, the more vicious the cross-examination. Like all trial lawyers, Dan dreaded having his star witness cross-examined while he was virtually powerless to intervene.

"Mr. Burleson, you have been very certain with your identification of my client, haven't you?"

"Yes."

"Very, very, very certain, aren't you?"

"He was the man," Burleson responded calmly.

"Perhaps you could describe his clothing. What was he wearing? Start with the shirt. What kind was it?"

"I'm not sure."

"Light or dark?"

"It struck me as being light, but I'm not sure."

"Now, did he have a coat or jacket on?"

This was standard defense cross-examination of an eyewitness. Question in detail about every conceivable fact. The witness had to say over and over that he wasn't sure. This almost never made a difference to the jury. They understood how anyone could recognize a person who committed a crime against them but not recall every detail of the event. Nonetheless, Dan was concerned because Hair was very skillful and was doing a much better job than most defense attorneys. Dan listened as Hair went on for two full hours. He peppered Burleson with question after question about clothing, hair, when the various men had shaved, and every detail Hair could dream up.

After what seemed like an eternity, Hair concluded sarcastically, "'I'm not sure' seems to sum up your testimony, Mr. Burleson."

"Objection." Dan was happy for a chance to interrupt. "That's an argument, not a question."

"Sustained." Judge Hamilton agreed with Dan.

Hair smiled at the judge. "I was done anyway. Pass the witness."

Dan was ready. A broad smile crossed his face.

"As you were being beaten, dragged from your car, fitted with a sack over your head, and screamed at about not obeying the Ku Klux Klan, I imagine you were very careful to note whether any of these criminals were pigeon-toed and the color of their socks?"

The courtroom exploded into laughter. Judge Hamilton began striking his gavel. At the same time Hair rose to his feet shouting his objection. "We might as well be tried on a river bottom as with this crowd!"

"I will not tolerate a circus atmosphere in my courtroom!" Hamilton spoke loudly. "Mr. Hair, your comment is not appropriate. It appears to me that the spectators are about evenly divided in their sympathies and they were all laughing. Even district attorneys say things that some find funny. We are going to have a fair, orderly trial. Now proceed, Mr. Moody."

Dan knew he had neutralized two hours of cross-examination in a few seconds. He wanted to finish and get to his next witness.

"Your testimony then is that you can remember

the defendant's face but not the details of his clothing?"

"Yes, sir, I'm a salesman. I've got to remember faces. I've always been considered by lots of people as being mighty good at it. I had occasion to remember the defendant's face. I got a clear impression of it. It certainly made an impression on me."

Dan's next witness, Gus Reno, was a friend of the defendant. Reno was a volunteer fireman from Taylor who had some devastating support for Burleson's testimony.

After the preliminary questions, Dan asked "Did you see your friend, Murray Jackson, on Easter Sunday of this year?"

"Yes, sir."

"When and where?"

"At my house around 11 A.M."

"Who was he with?"

"Olen Gossett."

"Were they on foot or travelling by vehicle?"

"It was Olen's Overland truck."

"Did the defendant, Murray Jackson, need something? Ask to borrow something?"

"Yes, he asked to borrow a pistol."

"Did he say why he wanted it?"

"Just that he needed it and would return it when he was done."

"Did you give him the pistol?"

"Yes, sir."

"Did he ever return the pistol?"

"Yes, that same day. He came by in the evening."

"Was it dark already?"

"It had been dark for a while. Maybe an hour or two."

"Did he tell you what he had done with the pistol or how he used it?"

"No."

"Did it smell like it had been fired?"

"No, it looked like it did when I gave it to him."

"So by after dark on Easter Sunday, Murray Jackson had 'used' your pistol for whatever purpose he needed it for that day?"

"Apparently so."

"Pass the witness," said Dan.

Hair stood up. "No questions of this witness, your honor."

Dan could scarcely believe his ears. Reno had placed the defendant with Olen Gossett in an Overland truck and with a pistol that he needed for only the afternoon. Dan remembered how excited he was when Louis Lowe had first told him about this witness. Now, the defense was letting his testimony stand unchallenged. It was then Dan knew for sure Hair had a surprise witness.

Dan's next six witnesses went as he had planned. Jim Dillinger, a student at Taylor High School who knew Murray Jackson, testified he saw Jackson, Gossett, and Dewey Ball riding in the Overland truck on Easter Sunday afternoon.

Arthur Lyons testified. He was also a Taylor fireman who was a friend of the defendants. On Easter Sunday evening, Lyons had helped saw off the chain from around Burleson's neck. He then had gone to the Just a Bite Cafe where he saw Murray Jackson. He testified, "Jackson had a large spot or stain on his cap. It was black like some kind of paint or oil or tar."

B. F. Standifer testified he was a tailor and that Murray Jackson brought some clothing in the day after Easter and asked him to remove some black stains from them. Standifer testified that he wasn't sure what the stains were but that they could have been tar.

Dr. Zorn testified about the injuries he observed when he treated Burleson. Two more witnesses added some details about seeing the Overland truck and another car driving too fast from Jonah to Taylor about the time that Burleson was abducted.

By early afternoon, Dan was ready for a break. Harry Graves did the questioning of Fannie Campbell. She again told the story of the Klan notice and the abduction. There were some differences between her recollection and Burleson's but they were minor. On cross-examination, Hair was much more restrained than he had been with Burleson. He again went through her testimony and asked her to describe details, forcing her to answer that she was uncertain or not sure. But her identification of Jackson, Gossett, and Dewey Ball as being three of the four men with guns remained unshaken.

Dan called Louis Lowe as his final witness. Lowe testified that he was the constable of the Taylor area and had twenty-five years' experience in law enforcement. Lowe testified about being called to Mrs. Harbor's boarding house, about seeing Burleson, about the doctors coming to treat him, and about how Lowe and the others sawed the chain from his neck and used four jars of coal oil to get most of the tar off Burleson's face and hair.

Lowe also testified about his investigation. He told of finding the place outside of Taylor where the flogging had taken place. "It was a tree used as part of a fence. Barbed wire ran from it in both directions. There was blood on the ground around it and it looked like a lot of footprints. It was about a half mile west from the Taylor City Hall out in the country near Buttermilk Hill."

Dan wanted one final detail from Lowe. "You know, constable, there has been testimony that an Overland truck was seen along with a Ford car heading from Jonah back towards Taylor at about the time this crime occurred?"

"Yes, sir."

"And you know that R. W. Burleson testified he was put in an Overland truck after he was beaten and the truck drove him to City Hall where he was chained to the tree?"

"Yes, sir."

"Constable, are you familiar with the people and cars in Taylor?"

"Yes, sir. Lived there all my life. I reckon I know everyone and darn near everything that goes on in Taylor.

"How many motor vehicles are there in Taylor?"

"Several hundred. The number grows every year."

"What are the most popular brands?"

"In Taylor, you can only buy Fords and Dodges, so that's what everyone has."

"What about the Overland Company?"

"No, we don't see many of theirs in Taylor."

"Are there any?"

"Yes, sir. There is one truck."

"Who owns it?"

"Olen Gossett."

After a brief cross-examination, Lowe was excused.

Dan stood up. "The State rests, your honor."

Hair began the defense by recalling Fannie Campbell. "After you left Weir on Easter Sunday, your first stop was the cemetery to visit your husband's grave?" Hair asked, repeating an earlier question. Mrs. Campbell again testified she was sure.

Hair then recalled Burleson. "You are absolutely certain that when you left Weir on Easter Sunday you made no stops until you got to Jonah?" Burleson said he was sure.

Dan knew it was a small discrepancy. Witnesses

remember what is most important to themselves. He also knew jurors seldom paid much attention to such discrepancies. But he had never seen a defense attorney make such dramatic use of such a small detail. By recalling the state's two key eyewitnesses at the beginning of the defense case, Hair had really emphasized the difference in the testimony. He now knew why W. W. Hair had such an excellent reputation.

Hair began to call witnesses. The first half dozen witnesses had attended a party in Circleville on Easter evening. They all testified they saw the defendant at the party. However, none of them saw him before 8:30 P.M. Dan carefully cross-examined the witnesses to establish that Circleville was a short drive from Taylor and that the defendant had plenty of time to commit the crime around 6:30, leave Burleson tied up at Taylor City Hall around 7:30, and be at a party that was at most fifteen minutes away by 8:30. Sheriff Lee Allen and Constable Louis Lowe had learned of the party early in their investigation, and there were no surprises in the witnesses' testimony.

Hair then called a dozen character witnesses. They all testified that Murray Jackson had a good reputation for being a law-abiding citizen and that he was a combat veteran of World War I. Since Jackson didn't really have a bad reputation, Dan carefully limited his cross-examination.

Hair then called witnesses to establish alibis for Sam Threadgill and Chief Bob Hewlitt, both of whom had been arrested for this crime but not indicted.

Dan wasn't sure whether the alibi witnesses were being truthful or not. But he didn't want to divert the jury's attention from Murray Jackson, so he limited his cross-examination of these witnesses to one basic question. "You testified before the grand jury and based upon all the evidence the grand jury heard, no indictments were returned against either Sam Threadgill or Bob Hewlitt?"

Dan was taking a bit of a risk by not challenging the alibi witnesses more. He knew for sure that Bob Hewlitt's witnesses were lying, but he didn't want to move away from Murray Jackson, and he didn't want to tip off his cross-examination tactics in case Hair's surprise was a really good alibi witness for Jackson.

Just as Dan was finishing his cross-examination of the last alibi witness for Hewlitt, he looked down on the table. County Attorney Evans had written a note: "We have a problem. Get a recess. Quickly!"

Dan was able to get a recess. The prosecution team, all seven lawyers plus Sheriff Allen and Constable Lowe, gathered in the county attorney's office.

Evans explained that an unknown man who was acting like a witness had been hanging out in the courthouse rotunda for the past hour. "I tried to talk to him but he said he would talk only if Mr. Hair or Senator Wood said it was okay."

"Louis, Lee, have you seen him?" asked Dan.

"I have," Lowe replied. "He won't talk to me, either, but I'm pretty sure I know who he is. He's one of the Prewitt boys from Granger. They run a grocery store there."

The men all started talking at once.

"Okay, okay. No need to panic," said Dan. "We all expect a surprise witness and the most likely defense they would have is some alibi for where Jackson was at 6 or 6:30. Let's listen to his testimony and then, Louis and Lee, you can spend the weekend looking for rebuttal witnesses. Let's get back into the courtroom."

It was the middle of Friday afternoon. The courtroom remained packed with spectators. Judge Hamilton allowed the men to remove their suit coats each day at noon. The courtroom windows were all open, and the ceiling fans were working overtime. But the combination of the 90-degree September afternoons and the body heat of four hundred people was making the room unbearable.

As everyone reassembled from the recess, the jurors, lawyers, and spectators all were beginning to look weary. All but one defense attorney. W. W. Hair had a smile on his face and a gleam in his eye. He was about to call his twenty-ninth witness of the day, the one he had been saving.

"The defense calls Porter Prewitt to the stand."

The courtroom was perfectly still as all eyes focused on the twenty-three-year-old man from Granger who took the oath and answered questions about his name and that he ran a grocery and hardware store in downtown Granger.

Hair moved to his point. "Mr. Prewitt, what were you doing on Easter Sunday afternoon?"

"I was at my store catching up on my books, doing the accounting work."

"What time did you leave work?"

"It was five in the afternoon when I left. I went home, took a bath, dressed for the evening, and came back to downtown."

"Where did you go?"

"I went into the Corner Drug Store. I bought a cold Coke and a pack of cigarettes."

"Did you see anyone you knew?"

"As I was leaving, two friends, Murray Jackson and Olen Gossett, were walking in."

"Did you talk to them?"

"We said our hellos, shook hands. Probably talked for five minutes."

"What did you do then?"

"I left. Murray and Olen went on into the drug store."

"Do you know how long they stayed?"

"I don't have any way of knowing."

"And what time was it when you first saw them?"

"It was six o'clock. I remember looking at my watch right as I was leaving the store, so that's right before I saw them."

"And then you talked with them for at least five minutes."

"Yes, sir."

"Pass the witness."

Dan knew he had little hope of breaking the witness down on cross-examination. But he knew that he had to make sure the jury knew that Dan didn't believe the witness. His questions were going to be hostile, aggressive, and loud. He was going to treat Porter Prewitt like the liar he was.

"Mr. Prewitt, you know Judge Critz and Mr. Graves sitting here, don't you?"

"Yes, sir."

"Known them all your life, haven't you?"

"Yes, sir."

"When they asked to speak to you in the rotunda a few minutes ago, you refused to even talk to them, didn't you?"

"Didn't know that I had to."

"You told them, you could only talk if Senator Wood okayed it?"

"Yes."

"Does Senator Wood own your testimony? Does he have some special claim on it?"

"Objection!" Hair jumped out of his chair.

"Sustained," Judge Hamilton shot back. "Mr. Moody, don't make personal attacks on the defense attorneys."

Dan changed his line of questioning. "You are testifying here willfully and deliberately, are you not?"

"I guess."

"You know what you are doing?"

"Yes."

"You understood the oath you took? You do know what telling the truth means?"

"Of course."

"It doesn't mean making things up, telling stories —"

"Objection!" shouted Hair. "That's an argument not a question."

"Sustained. Mr. Moody, questions please."

Dan continued. "Now, you are aware that everyone in the county, actually everyone in the state and most of the country, is talking about this trial?"

"I imagine."

"And here you are, a twenty-three-year-old grocer in Granger, Texas, with vital information that, if true, means we are trying the wrong man for the crime?"

"Wrong man, yes. That's right . . ."

"And you told no one about this before your testimony here today?"

"Oh, I told a few people."

"Like who?"

"Senator Wood. I told him. And I talked with my brother, Cecil. Said to him, no way could Murray and Olen have done it."

"You know Constable Lowe and Sheriff Allen?"

"Yes, sir."

"Did you ever tell them?"

"No."

"You know Judge Critz and Harry Graves?"

"Yes, sir. I see them around Granger from time to time."

"Did you ever tell them?"

"No, sir."

"Did you ever come tell me?"

"No."

90

"Or ask to testify to the grand jury?"

"No."

"You and the defendant are friends, are you?"

"We know each other."

"Did you visit him in jail?"

"No."

"When did you first talk to him about your testimony?"

"Last summer. He came to see me when he got out of jail."

"So you have important information on the most talked about case in the history of Williamson County and the only people you tell it to are the defendant, his lawyer, and your brother, is that right?"

"I'm telling you what I know."

"Mr. Prewitt, are you a member of the Ku Klux Klan?"

"Objection!" Hair was screaming as he rose. His face turned red. "The Klan has nothing to do with this case. The district attorney doesn't like this testimony, he doesn't want to — "

"He's making a jury speech!" Dan shouted.

Both of the lawyers were shouting simultaneously. The strain of the week-long trial had them both at the breaking point.

"Stop it!" cautioned Judge Hamilton. "I have already ruled on this issue. If the Klan or any other organization comes up as part of the evidence, it is a proper question. However, Mr. Moody, you will calm down and simply ask your questions. Proceed."

"Are you a member of the Invisible Empire, Knights of the Ku Klux Klan, Mr. Prewitt?"

"I've told the truth, Mr. Moody."

"Well, then, answer my question."

"Murray Jackson was with Olen Gossett in Granger talking with me in front of the Corner Drug Store at 6 o'clock Easter Sunday afternoon."

"Are you a member of the Ku Klux Klan?"

"I belong to several groups, Mr. Moody, that are none of your business."

Dan didn't care if Prewitt ever answered the question. By now, everyone in the courtroom knew he was a member of the Klan. Dan shifted his questioning. "Did you contribute money to the defense of this case?"

"That makes no difference in my testimony."

"Just answer the question."

"Yes, I gave fifteen dollars. I knew they weren't guilty, and I wanted to help."

Dan knew he had done as good a job as possible with his cross-examination. It was time to stop.

"No more questions." Dan sat down.

"Gentlemen, it is getting late. We will resume tomorrow morning at 8:30 A.M. Tomorrow is Saturday, and we will work as late as need be to try to finish with the defense," Judge Hamilton announced.

Later, the prosecution team was meeting in the county attorney's office. They were all exhausted after five days of trial. They discussed their strategy for Saturday and what other witnesses the defense would call. They all felt Dan's cross-examination had been effective.

Judge Critz observed, "About half the spectators believed Prewitt and thought your cross-examination was rude and obnoxious. The other half thought that Porter Prewitt lied about everything but his name and that you were too easy on him."

"That, of course, is our problem," explained Dan. "We can't take a chance that one or more of the jurors is looking for a reason to doubt and looking through Klan eyes. We need something concrete to refute the alibis."

Sheriff Lee Allen said, "Now, we know that Jackson and Gossett were in Jonah from at least 5 or

5:30 because they had to be waiting on Burleson. They couldn't possibly have been in Granger at 6. But Porter Prewitt probably was in Granger."

Dan snapped his fingers. "Yes. Louis and Lee, you need to get up to Granger and find out what Prewitt really did Easter afternoon. There's bound to be someone who saw him or talked to him. I know I've already asked a lot of you, but stick with it till you come up with something." Dan smiled. "Our whole case depends on it. Good luck."

On Saturday morning the one surprise witness turned into a whole pack. Cecil Prewitt, Porter's brother, testified that he saw the defendant and Olen Gossett leaving the Corner Drug Store in Granger about 6:20. The drug store owner testified that he saw Porter Prewitt talking to Olen Gossett and Murray Jackson at his store around 6:00. Then two witnesses who were army buddies of Murray Jackson testified they saw Jackson and Gossett driving towards Taylor by themselves sometime around 6:30. Still another witness testified that he met the defendant at 7:30 in Taylor and then went together to the party at Circleville. In all, Hair called nine witnesses whose testimony, if the jury believed it, provided an iron-clad alibi for the defendant.

Dan was careful with his cross-examination on Saturday. While he had been aggressive and showed anger with Porter Prewitt, he remained much more professional with the eight other witnesses. He carefully asked each witness who they had talked to about their testimony. In each case, they admitted they had told no one except the defendant or one of his attorneys. Dan emphasized that if they had really had important information in the case they would have come forward and told the grand jury or some official. None of the witnesses had a good explanation for not coming forward earlier.

Dan was becoming increasingly worried about the alibi with each witness Hair called. One or two witnesses lying for a friend was one thing, but this was nine witnesses. Dan knew he needed to tie the Klan back into the case, but he would have to wait and hope. Perhaps the next witness, Tom Brown, would give him the opening he was looking for.

Brown testified that he had known the defendant since they served together in the army. He and another army friend, Hatton Nelson, were driving through Taylor after 6 P.M. on Easter Sunday and testified that not far north of Taylor, he passed a car with Gossett and Jackson heading south towards town. Hatton Nelson had testified to the same thing earlier.

Dan remembered that the name "Tom Brown" was on the list of probable members of the Taylor Klan that Louis Lowe had given him. The cross-examination followed the usual line. Dan got him to admit he had talked to only the defense attorneys about the case and that while his friend was charged with a horrible crime that he knew someone else must have done, he did not talk to anyone in authority about his knowledge.

"Do you have an interest in the outcome of this case?" Dan continued.

Brown didn't answer immediately. Finally, he said, "No."

"It took you a long time to answer, Mr. Brown. It doesn't take that long to answer when you are telling the truth."

Hair sprang out of his chair. "Objection. That's not a question."

"Sustained. Mr. Moody, stick to questions. Proceed," said Judge Hamilton.

"Why did it take so long to answer a simple question?" asked Dan.

Again Brown hesitated. "I thought I would take my time and study whether I have an interest or not."

Dan sensed that Brown would fluster easily and that he was not comfortable telling these lies. This was exactly the witness Dan was waiting for. He pressed on. "Isn't it a fact, that you are a member of the Ku Klux Klan?"

Again, Brown hesitated, "Yes, I'm a Klansman."

Dan could scarcely believe he had a Klansman on the stand making that admission. He walked over to his table and retrieved a sheet of paper. He would use it in a few minutes. He remained standing by the counsel table and asked again, "You are a member of the Invisible Empire, Knights of the Ku Klux Klan?"

"I said I was."

"And do you know that Murray Jackson also is a member?"

Hair and Wood were both out of their chairs shouting their objections. "I can't believe it. He is trying my client for membership in an organization, not a crime," finished Hair.

"Mr. Moody, I've given you latitude on the Klan issue, but you must have something specific to tie this question in with your cross-examination."

"I do, your honor. I'm showing that he does in fact have an interest in the case."

"I'll overrule the objection and allow you to proceed, but make sure you show a specific reason for asking this question and do it now."

"Thank you, your honor." Dan turned again to Tom Brown. "Is Murray Jackson also a member of the Ku Klux Klan?"

"I've heard that he is."

"Heard? Come now, surely you must have seen him at meetings, been out there burning crosses with him while you all were hiding underneath your robes?"

"There's no hiding, Mr. Moody." Brown was becoming more agitated, which was exactly what Dan wanted.

"You've seen him out at your meetings?"

"Yes."

"And from that you know, not just heard, but know he's a fellow member of the Klan?"

"Yes."

Dan turned his head from the witness and looked directly at the jury as he asked his next question. "Did you take an oath as part of becoming a member of the Klan?"

"Yes."

"And the oath says you are to engage in Klanishness with your fellow Klansmen. That includes doing business with Klansmen and not with anyone else?"

"We respect each other as honest business people. No crime in that."

Dan turned from the jurors, looked at the piece of paper he held, then looked at the witness, "Your oath says you will keep the secrets of your fellow Klansmen?"

"Yes."

"And you will keep these secrets except in the case of 'treason, rape, malicious murder or a violation of this oath' is what it says?" Dan read from the paper.

"Something like that."

"And you also promise to aid your fellow Klansmen, in this oath, don't you?"

"Yes."

Dan again turned to the jury. "So, as long as you're not committing treason, rape, malicious murder or violating your Klan oath, it's fine to come to the aid of your fellow Klansmen," Dan's voice thundered. He turned to look at Brown.

"I don't understand it exactly that way."

"Well, is it wrong to commit burglary?"

"Yes."

"But that's not one of the crimes excepted in the Klan oath, is it?"

"I guess not."

"Is it wrong to steal? You Klansmen know that, don't you?"

"Yes."

"But that's not one of the crimes excepted in your oath, is it?" Dan was now thundering every question. He was back to the emotional peak he had been when he questioned Porter Prewitt on Friday.

"I guess not. But no one understands the oath like you're making it out. We don't do those things." Brown was beyond agitation. He knew he was hurting the defense, but he didn't know how to respond.

"Well, what about perjury, you know, coming into court and lying? Is that something you know is wrong?"

Brown didn't respond.

"There's nothing in your oath that excepts perjury when you are helping out a fellow Klansman, is there?" Dan waited. "Is there, Mr. Brown?"

"I guess not."

"What about whipping people? Nothing in your oath about that?"

"No."

"What about beating a man over the head with a pistol? That's wrong, isn't it?"

"Yes."

"Nothing in your oath about that, either?"

"No."

Dan paused for a minute before his final question. He regained his composure, looked down and studied the paper he held, and motioned towards it as he began his final question. He lowered his voice from the near shout he had been using. "Mr. Brown, this oath you took obligates you to lie, steal, cheat, do anything but murder, rape, or treason, to come to the aid of Murray Jackson, your fellow Klansman, and yet you still expect someone to believe you?"

"Yes."

"Pass the witness."

The defense attorneys continued to call witnesses. None of them would admit to being Klan members and none of them would admit contributing to the defense fund. Dan resumed his careful, less emotional cross-examination style. By mid-afternoon, the defense had called their last of thirty-six witnesses.

As the last defense witness testified, Evans handed Dan a note. It read, "Allen and Lowe are waiting in the office. They have smiles on their faces and two witnesses for you to talk to."

"Mr. Moody, do you have any rebuttal?" asked Judge Hamilton.

"If we may have a brief recess, I'll let the court know."

"Very well, court is in recess for twenty minutes."

The sheriff and constable had every reason to be smiling. After a brief conference with the two witnesses, Dan was back in the courtroom, ready to proceed with rebuttal.

"The State calls Newell Cook," Dan announced.

Cook was a twenty-four-year-old country boy. He testified that he lived in Taylor. Dan got right to the point. "What were you doing Easter Sunday afternoon?"

"My girlfriend and I went for a ride in the country and then went up to Granger to meet another couple."

Dan heard activity at the defense table. They

were all whispering at once. Dan, who had spent months worrying about the defense's surprise witness, was happy to be returning the favor.

"Who is your girlfriend?"

"Ethel Pipkin."

"And who was the couple you met?"

"Porter Prewitt and his girlfriend."

"Are you and Porter Prewitt friends?"

"Yes, sir. I've known him for most of my life."

"What time did you meet Porter that afternoon?"

"Around 3 or 3:30."

"What was he doing?"

"Just what the rest of us were doing. We talked, drove around the countryside, and then went back to Lucille's house."

"Who is Lucille?"

"Oh, Lucille Ray, she's Porter's girlfriend."

"So you young people were out socializing on a pretty Sunday afternoon?"

"That's about it."

"Did Porter ever stop by his grocery store to work on his books or for any reason?"

"No, not while I was with him. I don't know what he did before I got there."

"How long did you spend with Porter?"

"The four of us were together all day. Or I guess all afternoon and evening."

"What time did you and Miss Pipkin leave?"

"Oh, it was late. We had dinner and didn't leave till around ten."

"It was after dark when you left?"

"Oh, well after dark. Ten o'clock would be my best recollection."

"From the time you hooked up with Porter and Miss Ray until you left around ten, were you together the whole time?"

"Yes, sir."

The defense cross-examination was minimal. They could guess who Dan was going to call next, and they knew they were going to have to talk with their witnesses to see how they were going to attack this testimony.

Dan didn't disappoint the defense. The next witness was Ethel Pipkin. Miss Pipkin's testimony was the same as her boyfriend's. The couple had met with Porter and his girlfriend around three on Easter afternoon and stayed together until late that evening.

Dan and his prosecution team called a series of short witnesses to rebut specific points made by the defense. By the time they were done, it was early evening. Everyone in the courtroom was exhausted from six straight days of trial. Dan closed his rebuttal, and Judge Hamilton announced that the defendants would have their last chance to call their own rebuttal witnesses on Monday.

He recessed court until Monday afternoon. "We can finish with any further defense witnesses and take care of any other legal issues. We can then have the lawyers make their arguments to the jury on Tuesday."

Dan was up early on Sunday. He went to church and taught his Sunday school class. Church and Sunday school were a welcome change of pace from the crude and violent world he was exposed to in his prosecution work.

Sunday afternoon, Dan caught up on some much needed sleep. He was up early on Monday, stopped by his office in the Travis County Courthouse, and headed north to Georgetown.

He wasn't sure if the defense would call any more witnesses. He thought briefly that they might take a risk and put Murray Jackson on the stand. But that would be a disaster. Jackson could only repeat testimony that the nine alibi witnesses had already given.

And Dan would be able to cross-examine about the pistol he borrowed and about his Klan membership. No, Hair would never allow Dan that opportunity.

Court resumed at 1 P.M. Hair announced that they had several witnesses. Dan looked over at Harry Graves, who had been in the rotunda and was now sitting down. Graves wrote on a piece of paper, "They have at least seven witnesses outside."

Hair's first witness was Frank Williams. Williams testified that he was a customer of the Prewitt's grocery store, that he paid for some groceries on the Saturday before Easter, but picked them up Sunday at 5 P.M.

"Was the store open?" asked Hair.

"No, but I knocked on the door in the back. Porter came and let me in. Helped me get the box with my groceries."

"And that was what time?"

"Five o'clock, Easter Sunday afternoon."

Dan's turn for cross-examination came sooner than he expected. Here was still another witness to support the alibi, and Dan knew the Klan issue was his best argument to convince the jury that all ten witnesses were lying. Dan went directly to the matter, "Are you a member of the Ku Klux Klan?"

"Yes, sir."

"You live out on Frank Wilkins's place, his farm, don't you?"

"Yes."

"And Frank Wilkins plays a big role in the local Klan, doesn't he?" Dan was guessing, but he knew Wilkins and assumed he did.

"Frank is the Cyclops."

"You mean the head Klansman for all of Taylor?"

"Yes, sir. There are a lot of people in the Klan, Mr. Moody. Lots of us are fed up with what's going on. We have doctors, lawyers, preachers, and every other type in the Klan. Some of your friends and neighbors are in the Klan. We raise money to help widows."

Dan knew that Hair had prepared Williams. He was answering Dan's questions by making a speech to the jury. After all, they, too, had friends and neighbors who were bound to be Klansmen. Dan was going to have to fire his questions rapidly and cut Williams off before he made any more speeches. "And you also took an oath to help your fellow Klansmen?"

"Yes."

"And that oath excepted only rape, treason, malicious murder, and violation of the Klan oath from the list of things you won't do to aid your brother Klansman?"

"No one understood it that way."

"But that list doesn't include perjury, does it?"

"Well —"

"And it doesn't include hitting a man on the head with a pistol?"

"No."

"And it doesn't include flogging a man?"

"No."

Dan passed the witness. Hair called two more witnesses to contradict some minor details of the state's witnesses. He then called Grady DeGlandon.

DeGlandon testified that he was a friend of Murray Jackson. He had seen Jackson and Olen Gossett together at 6:40 on Easter in Taylor. They had been alone. He was the eleventh witness to testify to facts that, if the jury believed them, made the defendant not guilty.

Dan was losing his patience with the defense. He decided to go directly to the Klan issue. He assumed Hair had the witness ready to make some speeches about the virtues of the Klan. The jury already knew about the oath, so Dan decided to take a chance with a new question.

"Are you a member of the Invisible Empire, Knights of the Ku Klux Klan?"

"Yes, sir."

"And so is Murray Jackson?"

"Yes, sir."

"And so is Olen Gossett?" There hadn't been any testimony about Gossett being in the Klan, and Dan didn't know whether he was or not.

"Oh, yes. He was one of our first members."

"Hmmm." Dan went fishing, "Is he an officer or anything?"

"Yes, he's the Klaliff."

"You mean Olen Gossett is the vice president of the Taylor Klan?" Dan tried to contain his surprise. He could tell from the amount of noise at the defense table that this was not the way they had prepared DeGlandon for cross-examination.

"You mean the same Klan that posted a five hundred-dollar reward if anyone could prove they were involved had their members and their Klaliff participate in this crime?"

"Mr. Moody, Olen Gossett didn't do this crime. The Klan doesn't do crimes. The Klan is growing stronger and stronger, and we —"

"Mr. DeGlandon," Dan interrupted. He knew this was something Hair wanted the witness to blurt out. Dan seized on the last words, though. "Stronger and stronger? When was your last initiation?"

"Just this last Friday night."

The courtroom buzzed with whispers. As Dan was trying the Klan in court, their numbers were still growing.

Dan stood up, looked at the jury. They were all stone faced, not portraying any emotion. He was going to have to trust them. "Pass the witness."

Hair asked for a recess. Dan and the other lawyers guessed that Hair was not happy with the afternoon's testimony. The defense now had eleven alibi witnesses before the jury. But they would not be happy with still more Klan testimony.

Court resumed. "The defense closes on rebuttal," Hair announced.

The courtroom again broke out into a series of loud whispers. The spectators clearly had not expected the defense to stop so soon. Judge Hamilton used his gavel to restore order.

"Gentlemen," he told the jury. "You have now heard all the evidence in the case. I will prepare the charge of the court, which I will read to you tomorrow morning. It will contain all of the instructions needed to reach a verdict. You will then hear arguments from the lawyers on both sides. I will allow each side four and a half hours. The district attorney goes first, then the defense next, and then the district attorney finishes. Court will stand in recess until 10 A.M."

As the other lawyers remained in the courtroom to discuss the judge's legal instructions to the jury, Dan slipped off to the relative quiet of the county attorney's office. Sheriff Allen soon joined him.

"You look exhausted, Dan."

"I'm sure we both are. We haven't had much time to really talk since the trial began."

"Something about six days of trial and a hundred witnesses that makes it difficult to have too much spare time."

"What really has me worried is, what if we lose? It's not only a failure for Dan Moody or Lee Allen, you know. It's a victory for the Klan. If we lose, when will the next sheriff and district attorney go after the Klan? Why would they even try?"

"You'll finish them off with your final argument tomorrow. You'll get your conviction," Lee predicted confidently.

"But to win, we need not only a conviction. We need a prison sentence. A hundred-buck fine and ten days in jail would be a Klan victory almost as much as a not guilty verdict."

Lee smiled encouragingly. "Don't worry. Your final arguments always get results."

The courthouse bell chimed ten when court convened the next morning. If the courtroom had been full for the first six days of trial, it was now far beyond capacity. Every seat was taken, the outside balcony was crowded, and the rotunda was full. Some of the overflow sat on the courthouse steps under the open window and still more milled around the courthouse lawn.

Judge Hamilton began reading his instructions to the jury. "Gentlemen, your verdict must be unanimous. You are to determine whether the district attorney has proven the defendant guilty beyond any reasonable doubt. If you find him guilty, you are also to determine his sentence somewhere between a minimum of a fine only and a maximum of five years in state prison."

Dan began by telling the jury that he had to prove that Murray Jackson had hit R. W. Burleson on the head with a pistol. He then outlined each of the ten witnesses he called. He emphasized that both Burleson and Mrs. Campbell had gotten a good look at the defendant, and they were positive he was the man. He also emphasized the testimony of Gus Reno.

"Mr. Reno was the defendant's friend, and he told you the defendant borrowed a pistol in the morning and returned it that evening. That's the right time frame for someone who was going to use the gun to assault Burleson."

Dan completed his opening statement in less than an hour. He ignored the defense witnesses. He would wait to attack them in his closing. He also wanted the jury to go to lunch and then listen to all four and a half hours of the defense arguments during the hottest portion of the day.

After lunch, Senator Wood began a very friendly, low-keyed explanation of the law. He reminded the jury, "We don't *guess* people into state prison. We require a high level of proof, almost certainty, proof beyond a reasonable doubt."

Wood then talked about Murray Jackson. "He's a boy who grew up in Taylor. Not much different than you or your kinfolks. And you heard from all sorts of people about his good reputation here in the community."

Hair took the opposite approach. He spent three and a half hours attacking every portion of the state's case.

First, he attacked the identification. "Eyewitnesses! Eyewitnesses!" he shouted. "What kind of eyewitnesses are these? This traveling salesman living with an attractive widow. Living there for weeks at a time. These people aren't reliable. They were too excited to know anything. They couldn't say if the men who assaulted them were wearing shirts or jackets, they didn't know if they were clean shaven, they didn't know, they didn't know, they didn't know . . ." Hair stopped for a long pause. ". . . they simply didn't know who assaulted them.

"And then you heard the rest of the story. Eleven, not one or two like the state's mistaken eyewitnesses, but eleven people came and told you Murray Jackson was in Granger at about the time of the crime and then went directly to Taylor. And eleven people, eleven local people just like you, came up and told you Murray Jackson was somewhere else."

Hair turned from the jury and looked directly at Dan. "This is a case that never should have been brought to trial, never ever, ever brought to trial." He turned back to the jury. "And remember, they arrested five people, had them handcuffed and taken to jail, based upon these sorry eyewitnesses. Two of those cases have now been dropped and the rest will be when you find Murray Jackson not guilty.

"Now Mr. Moody knows he doesn't have a case, knows it's falling apart, so he raises the issue of a secret society. Well, no secret society is on trial here. Murray Jackson is on trial. A young man who has his whole life in front of him. Murray Jackson did not commit this crime. Murray Jackson is innocent."

Dan began his closing argument right after supper. He had the entire evening.

Dan focused the jury back on the crime itself. He detailed and graphically described the abduction, the whipping, and the tarring. As he talked about the lashes splitting Burleson's skin while Murray Jackson and the others taunted him, tearful sobs came from the spectators.

Dan then went back to how certain the eyewitnesses were, and how they were backed up with the defendant's own friends testifying about the pistol and the Overland truck.

He then turned and looked directly at Hair and began, "And they say that I brought up a so-called 'secret society.' There is no 'secret society' in this case. The 'society' has a name. It's the Invisible Empire, Knights of the Ku Klux Klan. And that society is not a secret anymore. It has been exposed in this courtroom.

"Gentlemen, I didn't bring it up. The Klansmen that kidnaped, flogged, tarred, and chained Robert Burleson brought it up. They asked, 'Why didn't you obey?' 'Did you threaten twenty-one Ku Klux?' And they taunted him over and over as they beat him.

"And Murray Jackson was one of those Klansmen. He struck the first blow with the pistol on R. W. Burleson's head.

"Then they brought their eleven alibi witnesses. Where have they been since April first? The most talked about case in the county's history, and they kept quiet about it. Yes, eleven eyewitnesses, three of whom admitted to being fellow Klansmen. They took an oath, placed their hands on the Bible, and swore they would do anything, commit nearly any crime, to come to the aid of their fellow Klansman. And that's exactly what they did. They came in here and committed perjury to aid their fellow Klansman."

Dan's time was nearing an end. He was still worried about a Klansman on the jury, and he wanted to make a quick point. "Now, there's a rumor about a ringer on this jury. I don't believe it for a minute, but you'll know soon enough when you deliberate if one of your number is unreasonable —"

"Object," Hair shouted. "He's trying to intimidate the jury, your honor."

Judge Hamilton sustained the objection, ordered Dan to stop, and told the jurors to disregard the remark.

Dan was ready to conclude. He looked the jurors directly in the eye, one by one. He began quietly, "Gentlemen, your fathers or grandfathers moved to Texas for a better way of life. Before that, their fathers left Europe to come here for a better life. We all have a common set of beliefs. Beliefs concerning freedom, democracy, and orderly procedures according to law. The Ku Klux Klan wraps itself in an American flag and believes in none of our values. They give secret orders and, if you don't obey them, they will try you, convict you, and punish you on the side of a road as you are chained, helpless to defend yourself.

"There is a darkness upon America. It is a darkness caused by cowards. Cowards who meet in secret, hide underneath bed sheets, and take the law into their own hands. Cowards," Dan turned and pointed directly at Jackson, "such as this defendant. Because on Easter Day, Murray Jackson, with up to nine other Klansmen, committed a horrible crime. They pistol-whipped, kidnapped, flogged, tarred, and chained a man who had the courage to stand up to them.

"Today, you have a chance to be men of courage. You have a chance to say, 'Enough.' You have a chance to pierce the darkness of the Klan with the light of real justice. On behalf of the people of Williamson County, I ask that you return a guilty verdict against this defendant and sentence him to state prison."

The jury filed out into the small jury room directly behind the courtroom. It was 9:30 P.M. There was nothing left but to settle down and wait. Since it was already late, the spectators were guessing that the jury would work for a little while, recess for the night, and begin serious deliberation in the morning.

Dan gathered his prosecutors and investigators. He thanked them for all their hard work. "Whatever the verdict, you can all be proud that you put the best possible case together."

The men, all exhausted, began to loosen their ties and a set of dominoes soon appeared.

The bailiff appeared in the office doorway. "Mr. Moody."

Dan looked up.

"The jury knocked on the door. They have a verdict."

9

Judgment Day

The jury remained in their room until all the spectators found seats or places to stand. The attorneys had reassembled around their tables. Seven men at the defense table including the defendant. Seven men at the prosecution table.

The bailiff called the courtroom to order.

"Gentlemen," the judge spoke to the lawyers. "The jury has indicated they have a verdict."

Dan looked at his watch, 9:50. They had deliberated only twenty minutes. The jurors undoubtedly had made up their minds before entering the jury room. And each had made up his mind the same way.

"We have no idea what the verdict is," Judge Hamilton warned the crowd of spectators, "but whatever it is, there will be no outburst by anyone either for or against the verdict. Bailiff, bring the jury in, please."

"All rise," the bailiff commanded.

The twelve men filed into the jury box one by one. They were all working men, farmers, ranchers, merchants, and tradesmen. They gave no hint of their verdict.

"Be seated," commanded the bailiff.

"Mr. Foreman," Judge Hamilton directed his comment to the last juror who entered the courtroom. He was holding the five pages of instructions the judge had given the jury. "Have you reached a verdict?"

The foreman stood up. "Yes, your honor."

"Very well, hand it up here, please."

The courtroom was absolutely quiet. Four hundred people looked intently as the bailiff took the instructions from the foreman and handed them to the judge.

Judge Hamilton glanced through the five pages and turned it over to the back of the last page. "The defendant will please rise," he commanded.

Jackson stood with Hair on one side and Senator Wood on his other.

Judge Hamilton read:

"Georgetown, Texas, September 25, 1923. We, the jury, find the defendant guilty as charged in the indictment and assess his penalty at confinement in the state penitentiary for a term of five years. T. J. Caswell, Foreman."

A guilty verdict and the maximum prison sentence! Dan showed no hint of emotion as the sentence sunk in. The case that couldn't be won had been won. Dan felt the special satisfaction that comes to a prosecutor when he knows he has worked hard, defied the odds, and obtained justice.

It would be an hour later when Dan finally left the courthouse. He could scarcely recall exactly what transpired after the verdict. Judge Hamilton thanked the jury and formally sentenced Jackson. Jackson's lawyers would undoubtedly appeal the case, and Jackson would be freed on bond during the appeal. But at least for tonight, he would be in jail. Dan had been swarmed by well-wishers, eager to congratulate him on his victory. If there was anyone against the verdict, they must have left right away because Dan never saw them.

It was a week later that Dan was sitting in his Austin office, working hard to catch up on his cases, when the phone rang. It was Sheriff Allen.

"Dan, I got an anonymous phone call. A man, a very scared sounding man, said he needed to meet with you and me, had some important information about the Klan."

"What's his name?"

"He wouldn't give it. He wanted to meet out in the country."

"They wouldn't try to set us up?"

Lee snorted. "That's why I wouldn't agree to meet him anywhere but my office. He finally agreed but only after dark."

"If he's willing to come to us—"

"It's some crackpot waste of time. You know it. I know it."

"Did he ask for directions to your office?"

"No."

"Which means he's been there before. I'm getting curious."

After a pause, Lee said, "Me too."

"I'll leave after work," said Dan. "I should get there right after dark."

Dan and Lee were alone in the courthouse basement — the sheriff's office. What could be safer? The two men discussed several cases. They were interrupted by a sharp knock on the outside door. When Lee opened it, he and Dan instantly recognized the fat man in the doorway. K. C. Baker, the Weir barber.

"K. C., are you the one who called?" asked Lee.

Baker was sweating and looked as if he had not slept for several nights. "Sheriff, I need to come clean. Can we talk?"

Baker did not look like the same man who appeared before the grand jury five months ago. Then, he had confidently denied knowing anything about R. W. Burleson receiving a notice or about Reverend Davis or the Ku Klux Klan.

Baker spoke very nervously. "I want to tell the truth," he began. He explained how at a Klan meeting he brought up Burleson and Mrs. Campbell, how he talked to Reverend Davis, and how the next day, he gave Davis and two other men directions to Mrs. Campbell's house.

Baker broke down crying several times. "I never meant it to go this far," he sobbed. "I never even meant for Burleson to get hurt. I don't even know that he was doing anything wrong. I was listening at the Klan meeting and got caught up in it. I didn't mean it."

Lee wrote out a statement with what Baker told them. Baker signed it. "Just go home now, K. C. You did the right thing. The district attorney and I will decide what to do later. You go home and stay away from any Klansmen."

Baker composed himself, got up, and left Lee and Dan. They looked at each other as broad smiles crossed their faces.

"It worked," Dan said quietly with only a slight hint of triumph in his voice.

"It did, indeed, though I don't think ol' K. C. feels sorry for anything, not one way or the other."

"Do you suspect he's worried about going to prison one way or the other?"

"I suspect. I wonder how worried the others are?"

"We'll soon see if they start slinking in here in the dark of night to confess their sins."

"Maybe I should start inviting them in?"

"That might be most encouraging," said Dan. "Give me an update. I'd like to have at least one more witness lined up before we go to the grand jury."

Lee began his work the next day. Turned out some other witnesses also had been losing sleep. He found two more willing to cooperate.

In November Dan took the case to the grand jury. The following morning, the *Austin American* headline reported the result:

"Klan Preacher Indicted for Perjury."

Olen Gossett was the next Klansman to face trial. His trial began in January 1924. After two days of delay tactics and jury selection, Hair and Senator Wood asked for a meeting with Dan.

The lawyers had many sharp exchanges in the courtroom. But they respected each other's abilities, and they remained friendly outside the courtroom. "Gossett's ready to give up," Hair explained to Dan. "He wants to stay out of prison."

"If he wants to plead guilty, that's fine," replied Dan. "But there won't be any recommendation of a suspended sentence from the district attorney."

"Dan, you can't be so intense about everything," counseled Wood. "You already have the only prison sentence in the whole United States against the Klan. Now, you can have a second felony conviction."

"No." Dan stood his ground. "If he wants an agreement, it has to be for prison time."

There was a silence among the men. Dan knew he wasn't going to give in. He knew it was unlikely the jury would give Gossett the same maximum sentence Jackson had gotten, but Dan knew the only thing that would shake the Klan up, the only thing that had scared K.C. Baker into finally telling the truth, was prison time.

"How long?" Hair asked, finally breaking the silence.

Dan looked thoughtful.

Hair explained what Dan already knew, but it needed to be out in the open. "You aren't going to find two juries in a row to give the maximum sentence. Plus, Gossett has a lot better character witnesses than Murray Jackson."

"One year. One full year in prison."

"Now Dan, sixty days in jail will give you everything you want," Wood explained.

"One year."

Hair looked directly at Dan. If he was looking for any sign of indecisiveness, he didn't see it. "Okay, give me a minute with Gossett."

Judge Hamilton reconvened court. "Gentlemen, are we ready to proceed with jury selection?"

"Judge, we'd like to change our plea," Wood announced.

The lawyers took little time selecting twelve men to serve on the jury. They asked each one question. "If the defendant pleads guilty, will you find him guilty and return a sentence which both the district attorney and the defense have agreed is proper for the case?" Each of the jurors agreed.

Judge Hamilton asked Olen Gossett how he pled to the charges in the indictment.

"Guilty, your honor."

Dan called Robert Burleson to testify to the facts of the crime and identify Gossett as one of his assailants. The lawyers then explained their agreement for the sentence to the jury. The jury went back to the jury room for a few minutes and then returned to court with their verdict.

Judge Hamilton read it to the defendant. "We, the jury, find the defendant, Olen Gossett, guilty and set his punishment at one year in prison."

At lunchtime the next Thursday, Dan was in the county attorney's office going over last minute details of the perjury case against Reverend Davis with the other lawyers. After several delaying motions, a jury had been selected and Judge Hamilton had told Dan to begin presenting his case after lunch.

Sheriff Lee Allen entered. "I've got them all here." He meant all the witnesses likely to be called that afternoon. "Do you gentlemen know what's going on outside?"

Dan looked up from the witness list he was going over. "I imagine a big crowd is assembling."

"Big? It's huge. Every train coming up from Austin is full. There's over a thousand, maybe fifteen hundred out there. The courtroom is packed, the rotunda is full, and there are a hundred more on the east side under the balcony. Two or three times the size for Murray Jackson. There must be at least fifty reporters. They're from all over the country."

"Klan preacher on trial," Graves said with a smile. "It makes for a pretty sensational headline."

"And wait until they realize we're going to call enough Klansmen to start our own chapter," Dan added.

"Maybe we should call it Justice Klan No. 1," said Lee. The men all laughed.

"Okay, okay. Let's don't be overconfident. We have lots of work to do." Dan gathered his papers and started for the courtroom.

Lee's estimate of the crowd had been accurate. Dan and the other lawyers had to work their way slowly down the packed hall to reach the courtroom.

As the prosecutors took their place, Dan looked over at the defense table. It was a new set of lawyers. A. M. Felts from Elgin, the defendant's hometown, was the lead defense attorney. The defendant, barely in his twenties, sat next to Felts. A young woman and an older couple were talking with the defendant. Dan assumed they were his wife and parents.

Oh, yes. The defense would be playing up the defendant's youth and using his wife and parents to extract every ounce of sympathy from the jury.

Dan also took a quick glance at Davis, but his eye was drawn down. Dan quickly noted one thing. There

116

it was, hanging from Davis's watchpocket. A fiery cross on his watch chain. A ruby-studded, gold cross. A symbol of the Ku Klux Klan. And the defendant was displaying it in the courtroom. Was he taunting Dan?

The first seven witnesses went smoothly. Dan called some of the prosecutors and grand jurors who were present when A. A. Davis had told the grand jury that he did not deliver the notice.

D. L. Noble, the grand jury foreman, recalled for the jury that the defendant had specifically said "I am not the man. Gentlemen, you are mistaken in the man."

This statement was the basis of the perjury case. Now Dan had to prove it was false. He wasted no time.

"The State calls Dr. John Martin," Dan announced.

The witness was sworn in and took the stand.

"State your name, please."

"Dr. John Martin."

"How are you employed?"

"I'm a physician here in Georgetown."

"Are you a member of any secret societies?"

"Yes, sir. I'm a member of the Ku Klux Klan."

The courtroom burst into murmurs. Judge Hamilton gaveled it back to order.

"What position did you hold in the Klan?"

"I was the cyclops of Klan Number 178."

"That's the Georgetown chapter?"

"Yes, sir."

"Do you recall a meeting back last January 1923, where Reverend A. A. Davis was the speaker?"

"Yes, sir."

"What was his topic?"

"Anti-Catholic, the best I can remember."

"Was there a conversation about a situation in Weir?"

"Yes, sir. But I didn't want it brought up at the meeting, and I ruled it out of order."

"Did Reverend Davis say anything?"

"He said he'd see about it later or look into it. Something like that."

There was little cross-examination. Judge Hamilton recessed the case until the morning.

On Friday morning, Dan was ready to continue. If the crowd was stunned that the head of the local Klan would testify against a fellow Klansman, they were really going to be stunned today, thought Dan. Today, they were going to be spectators at a Ku Klux Klan parade.

Cornelius Beard was Dan's first witness.

"Are you a member of any secret societies?" Dan asked.

"Yes, sir. I'm in the Ku Klux Klan."

"Which chapter?"

"Number 178, Georgetown."

"Were you present at a meeting where Reverend A. A. Davis spoke?"

"Yes, sir."

Beard went on to relate how A. A. Davis met with K. C. Baker and himself after the meeting, and how Davis agreed to go look into the matter the following day. Again, there was little cross-examination from the defense.

Dan's next witness was K. C. Baker.

"Were you a member of any secret societies?"

"Yes, sir. I was a member of the Georgetown Ku Klux Klan."

"Do you remember testifying to the grand jury looking into the Burleson flogging?"

"Yes, sir."

"Did you tell them the truth?"

"No, sir."

"Did you lie?"

"Yes, sir."

"What did you lie to them about?"

"I told them I didn't know Reverend A. A. Davis."

"Do you, in fact, know him?"

"Yes, sir. I met him at a Klan meeting."

Baker went on to relate how he told Davis about Burleson, how Davis agreed to look into it, and how Davis showed up in his barber shop the next morning to get directions to Mrs. Campbell's.

"Why did you lie to the grand jury, Mr. Baker?"

Baker had been sweating heavily throughout his testimony. Judge Hamilton had instructed him several times to keep his voice up. Dan thought how pathetic Baker looked compared to the way he acted when he was lying to the grand jury.

"Why did you lie, Mr. Baker?" Dan repeated.

"I don't know," he finally said in a near whisper.

"Speak up, Mr. Baker," Judge Hamilton admonished. "The jury needs to hear you."

"I don't know," he repeated in a louder voice. "I guess I was afraid. I guess I was trying to protect the Klan."

Dan then called John McDaniel.

"I'm a student at Southwestern University."

"Are you a member of any secret societies?"

"Yes, sir. I'm a member of the Ku Klux Klan."

McDaniel told the jury he was on sentry duty the night Reverend Davis spoke to the Georgetown Klan. He had heard the conversation about Burleson after the meeting, and the next day he had gone with Davis and had been there when Davis delivered the warning.

"Mr. McDaniel, when Reverend Davis told the grand jury asking about the notice, when he told them 'I am not the man. Gentlemen, you are mistaken in the man,' was that the truth?"

"No, sir. I was with him. It would be a lie if he denied doing it."

Dan's final Klansman to testify was S. J. Purl, who testified that he was a Klansman and had lent

119

his car to Davis the day after the Klan meeting so that Davis could drive to Weir.

Dan called a few more witnesses and then called Robert Burleson to conclude his case. Burleson told the jury how A. A. Davis had delivered the warning to him in Weir. He recounted all the brutal details of the flogging.

"Do you see in the courtroom the man who delivered the Klan warning to you that day in Weir?"

"Yes, sir."

"Point him out, please."

"That's him," Burleson said as he pointed.

"That's the man?" Dan asked as he pointed at Davis.

"Yes, sir."

"And if he told the grand jury he wasn't the man?"

"If he told them that, he's a liar."

After Dan rested his case, A.M. Felts called Jim Abbott, the first of three defense witnesses.

"Mr. Abbott, are you acquainted with the defendant?"

"Yes, sir. He preaches at our church in the Shiloh community. It's a small church on the other side of Taylor near Thrall."

"Do you specifically recall Easter Sunday of last year, 1923?"

"Yes, sir. He preached the sermon that Sunday. His mother, father and wife came up from Elgin with him. He preached in the morning, came to my house for supper, and then we had church services again that evening."

A little confused, Dan looked over at Graves.

Graves leaned toward Dan and whispered, "I think they've given up."

That was the only thing that made sense, so Dan nodded his agreement. If the defense was concentrating on Easter Sunday, they were trying to show that Davis wasn't part of the flogging. They were conceding that he was guilty of perjury. The trial was really just about the sentence.

Graves leaned back towards Dan and whispered, "You better start working on your punishment arguments right now."

Again, Dan nodded his head in agreement. He needed to be careful with his cross-examination of Mr. Abbott. He might be telling the truth, although Dan strongly suspected Davis was one of the men in the second car that abducted Burleson.

Dan began his cross-examination. "Does Mr. Davis preach a good sermon?"

"Yes, he does a fine job."

"And his sermon on Easter Sunday. Was it about the Ten Commandments?"

"I don't recall exactly."

"Well, what about the Ninth Commandment, 'Thou shalt not bear false witness,' not lie. Was his sermon about lying?"

"Not that I remember."

"But he knows the commandments, and he knows that lying is wrong?"

"I'm sure he does."

Felts called Mrs. Jim Abbott and Mrs. A. A. Davis, who also testified that the defendant spent all day Easter in Shiloh. Felts then rested his case.

"Mr. Moody, do you have any rebuttal?" asked Judge Hamilton.

"No, sir."

"Then we will proceed with final arguments."

Graves argued the State's case first. He explained the law to the jury and then explained how they had proved that Davis lied to the grand jury. He concluded, "This is not a case for a suspended sentence. This defendant lied, he lied to protect his fel-

121

low Klansmen, he lied to prevent the truth from being revealed. You must send him to prison."

After the dinner recess, Felts began his final argument. He pointed out that the defendant was not charged with the flogging and did not participate in it. "You should reserve prison sentences for those men," he argued.

"My client is a very young man. He made a foolish mistake. I implore you, don't send him to prison. Please, take a look at his mother, take a look at his father, take a look at his wife. Think of their shame. My client, my client's family, will live all their lives with this shame. That will be their greatest punishment. Think of them. Think of their shame. Please suspend any sentence you impose."

It was now Dan's turn to close. Felts had made a very emotional speech. Dan was going to turn that emotion around.

"There has never been a blemish on the name of our county such as the one that was put here last Easter. On that day, in the name of hate, these cowards of the Klan beat Robert Burleson to a bloody pulp. But it was more than a beating. It was to be a public message that the Klan was all-powerful, that the Klan was above the law. And so, they took Burleson and chained him to a tree on the town square of Taylor. One of the most public places they could find. It was an act of defiance against you, gentlemen. Against everything you believe in.

"The sheriff, the constable, and the grand jury all conducted an investigation. By far, the most difficult of my career. Why? Because of lies. That investigation was thwarted at every turn by lies. By perjury, gentlemen. As Klansman after Klansman took an oath to tell the truth and then lied.

"But none was more blatant, none was more arrogant, than the defendant sitting in this courtroom. He, who instigated it all, he who delivered the warning to leave Weir, he who set this terrible action in motion, he lied to the grand jury. And everyone else lied to protect him.

"Mr. Felts asks you for mercy. Why? Why should there be mercy in this case?

"Gentlemen, every one of you knows about the Ku Klux Klan. You all know at least some of its symbols. Well, look at the defendant's watch chain. As he sits in this courtroom, as his lawyers ask for mercy, you see that he wears a gold cross studded with red rubies. The fiery cross symbol of the Ku Klux Klan. Still, he defies you."

All eyes on him, Davis stayed rock steady, the cross gleaming, its rubies sparkling.

"We are in a court of law. Here justice is dispensed through proper, orderly procedures. Into this courtroom comes the fiery cross that the defendant wears. It represents hate and contempt for order. These two cannot co-exist. America and her system of justice cannot co-exist with the Ku Klux Klan and its system of hate. In this courtroom today, you can extinguish the fire of the Klan's cross of hate and lift high the American system of justice.

"On behalf of the people of Williamson County, I ask that you find the defendant guilty of perjury and sentence him to time in prison."

The packed courtroom was perfectly still as Dan finished. After standing silently for a moment, he returned to his seat.

It was ten o'clock, and Judge Hamilton sent the jury out to deliberate. Any hope of a quick verdict was dashed when the jury asked to be taken to their dormitory for the night at ten thirty. Their deliberations would resume Saturday morning.

The prosecutors and Sheriff Lee Allen were sitting around in the county attorney's office, waiting for the crowd to disperse.

123

"I was hoping for another quick verdict," said Lee.

"Don't worry," responded Graves. "They don't want to send anyone so young to prison without thinking about it. A good night's rest, and we'll have a quick verdict in the morning."

Graves proved to be very insightful, because the following morning at eight-thirty, the jury began its deliberation, and at nine they knocked on the door.

"They have a verdict," announced the bailiff.

It took nearly half an hour for everyone to reassemble in the courtroom. It was again packed. Judge Hamilton warned against outburst and then had the jury brought back to the courtroom.

"Gentlemen, have you reached a verdict?"

"We have, judge," responded the foreman.

"Very well, pass it up."

The bailiff gave the papers to Judge Hamilton.

"The defendant will please rise," the judge instructed. Davis, who showed no emotion during the trial, stood with his lawyers.

Judge Hamilton read, "Georgetown, 1-26-1924. We, the jury, find the defendant, A.A. Davis, guilty of perjury as charged in the indictment and assess his punishment at two years in the state penitentiary. Signed Jack Jordan, foreman."

10

The Final Blow

Two weeks later, the phone in Dan's office rang. It was Harris Melasky.

"I wanted to congratulate you on your last conviction."

"Well, we thought Dewey Ball would do anything and everything to avoid trial," replied Dan.

"Yes, but Judge Hamilton is smart. When he sent those three doctors to Taylor to examine him to see if he was really sick, Dewey knew his goose was cooked."

"Yes, I think he was wise to take the one-year prison sentence."

"Well, four prosecutions and four Klansmen sent to prison. We knew you could do it, Dan. But what I really called about was the *Houston Chronicle*. Have you read what they wrote about you?"

"No. It was good, I hope."

"Good, yes, very good. They are enthusiastically ready to support you for attorney general. Dan, you need to decide about this attorney general race soon."

"I'm really busy, Harris. District attorney is a non-stop job."

"Well, let's get together. You, me, and Lee Allen, and we'll talk."

"Okay, fine, but it will have to be after work."

"Okay, I'll set it up for tomorrow night."

The three men, Harris Melasky, Lee Allen, and Dan Moody, met at the cafe in the Stephen F. Austin Hotel in downtown Austin the following night. The Stephen F. Austin, a tall hotel, was brand new, but its location just a short walk from the capitol and the courthouse instantly made it the unofficial political capitol of Texas state politics.

"Well, Harris, have you figured out my political future?" Dan began with a laugh.

"It's really up to you," Harris replied with a serious tone. "You defeated the Klan in the courtroom, you broke their code of secrecy, but the Klan isn't going away, if you notice. They will still be in power as long as they win elections."

Lee said, "The very day you got the conviction on Dewey Ball, they announced a mass initiation of up to 500 new members for the Austin chapter."

"And right now, they control the city hall and county courthouse in nearly every city in Texas," Harris said.

"But all that will change with this next election," said Dan. "All their violent acts and our convictions have discredited them."

"But we still need a good candidate to beat them," said Harris. "And right now, you are the most popular man in the state. The papers would love to take the high road by endorsing you. You really need to make this race for attorney general."

"And what are the Klan's plans for the election?" asked Dan.

"Same tactic as always," replied Harris. "They'll hold an elimination primary and put their support behind one candidate for each race."

"Harris, I'm only a country sheriff, I guess," interjected Lee. "What's this 'elimination primary?'"

"Just an informal poll. All three hundred Klan

chapters will vote on their favorite. Whoever gets the majority will be endorsed by the Klan and they'll vote nearly a hundred percent for him. That way they can ensure that their candidate will at least make a runoff by not splitting the Klan vote between four or five candidates."

"Who do you think will end up as their candidate for attorney general?" Dan asked Harris.

"Edward Ward from Corpus Christi has it locked up. The real fight is for the Klan endorsement for governor. There are at least three Klansmen who have announced. It seems the Houston Klan has one candidate and the Dallas Klan has another."

"Okay, so how does a poor boy from a small town get elected to a statewide office?"

"I'm not going to kid you, Dan," explained Harris. "You won't have much money. The campaign will mostly be you and your Ford driving from town to town. But you're well known, and the newspapers like you. I really think you can win."

"Meanwhile, the Klan candidate has lots of money and the organization of three hundred local chapters," observed Dan.

"Well, Dan, if you remember, I explained last summer to you how there was no way you could beat the Klan in court. And you told me that you had to try anyway. Well, you made a believer of me and everyone else in the state who believes in decency and order."

"You beat the Klan in court, you can beat them at the ballot box," added Lee.

"Okay, Harris, if I decide to run, what's the first step?" asked Dan.

"Just leave it to Lee and me," said Harris. "Hold off your announcement until the end of March. That way you will keep getting newspapers to encourage you to run and people will keep talking about you.

Then we'll have a big announcement here in Austin. I'll reserve the Senate chambers and arrange for a dozen or so politically important people to give short speeches for you. It will look great in the newspapers."

"And I'll organize the hometown folks in Taylor and Georgetown," added Lee. "We can get some special train cars and bring hundreds of your friends down to Austin for the announcement."

"And then what?" asked Dan.

"You let your friends around the state go to work for you, organize speaking engagements. About six weeks before the primary, you get in your Ford and start driving. You speak at every town meeting and political gathering we can find for you," said Harris. "You won't have much money so you'll have to shake as many hands as possible, talk to any group of two or more, and hope the newspapers give you maximum coverage."

"It's the only way to finish off the Klan," said Lee.

"And that's what we will do," said Dan. "We'll rid Texas of the Klan for good."

It was a hectic five months before the men would reunite at the Stephen F. Austin Hotel. The campaign had gone as predicted. There were four candidates for the Democratic nomination for attorney general. In Texas, in 1924, there wasn't much of a Republican party, so the Democratic nomination was a guarantee of victory in the general election.

Edward Ward, the Klan candidate, and Dan were clearly the front-runners. Dan had made his big announcement at the state capitol in March in front of a packed Senate chambers.

For the next six weeks, Dan drove from town to town. East Texas, North Texas, the Panhandle, West Texas, the Rio Grande Valley, the Gulf Coast, and back again. Anywhere he could find a political dinner, a church picnic, a newspaper reporter, a lunchtime crowd at the local cafe, Dan stopped. He shook hands and talked about how important it was to stop the Klan.

"Well, Dan, you look worn out," commented Lee as the men sat down to dinner.

"You can't really appreciate how big this state is until you drive it," said Dan. "It's 810 miles from Beaumont to El Paso and nearly as many miles from Amarillo to Brownsville, and I've driven every one of those miles several times."

The men laughed. "Yes, we've seen the newspaper reports," said Harris. "If your goal was to get free publicity, you are an overwhelming success."

"Will it pay off tomorrow?" Dan asked.

"Everyone says you're the front-runner," responded Harris. "The only question is will you have the fifty percent you need to avoid a run-off."

"Most people are talking about the governor's race," added Lee.

"As I know all too well," said Dan. "There are too many candidates in that race. There's bound to be a run-off."

"That's right," said Harris. "Felix Robertson won the Klan elimination primary, so he'll get all the Klan vote. That will get him into the run-off, and it looks like Lynch Davidson will be the anti-Klan candidate."

"Don't be too sure about Davidson. Ma Ferguson is gaining strength," said Dan.

"Texas will never elect her," said Lee. "She's just a front for her crooked, impeached, ex-governor husband."

"I feel the same way, but the Fergusons have their supporters, and Lynch and T. W. Davidson are dividing the votes of most decent Texans," said Dan.

"Well, let's don't worry about the governor," said Melasky. "It would be an absolute nightmare if we had the Fergusons versus the Klan as our choice for governor. It won't happen."

It was several days before the election results were known. On election night, it was clear that Dan had won a great victory, but it was unclear whether he had the fifty percent needed to avoid the run-off. But when the final results were in, they read:

Moody	49%
Ward	30%
Others	21%

Dan had fallen roughly 10,000 short of a victory without a run-off. But the governor's race had produced a surprise. The Klan candidate, Felix Robertson, finished first but had only twenty-eight percent of the vote. Ma Ferguson had finished second, barely edging out Lynch Davidson by 5,200 votes.

As local election results trickled in, it was clear that the Klan had suffered a huge setback. But, by using the elimination primary and giving only one candidate all the Klan votes, the Klan candidates were in the run-off.

The run-off primary was scheduled for late August, four weeks away. Dan resumed his campaign immediately. But it soon became obvious from the huge crowds supporting Dan that Edward Ward had no real support, except among the Ku Klux Klan. When the final results were in, Dan won by an overwhelming landslide:

Moody	463,411
Ward	211,783

All of the Klan candidates for statewide office lost. They also lost local elections in nearly every

Texas county. The Klan was dead as a political force in Texas.

"Congratulations, Dan," an excited Lee Allen greeted Dan. "You did it. You beat the Klan!"

Dan had finished up the race in Austin. He was at an election night party with his supporters. Even though there was still a Republican to beat in the general election, Dan, the Democrat, would easily beat any Republican. Dan's supporters were all jubilant. The long election was finally over. Dan was surrounded by well-wishers, giving him their congratulations, and he thanked each of them for their work in the campaign.

It was after midnight before Harris Melasky got Dan to sit down alone with him for a private conversation. Harris smiled, "You did it, Dan. Hard to believe only a few years ago we were opening a law office in Taylor with a borrowed typewriter and a wooden box for a desk."

Both men laughed. They had, indeed, come a long way. "I want you to enjoy your victory. But Dan, you are going to be facing an impossible situation as attorney general."

"How's that?" asked Dan.

"The Fergusons won tonight too. Do you remember why Jim Ferguson was removed from office?"

"We were awfully busy back then. We had just started our law office," explained Dan. "I don't remember all the charges, but he did some fancy bookkeeping to get the state to pay for some personal expenses, right?"

"Not only that," said Melasky. "He cooked up a bunch of other schemes. He also took state money and had it deposited in the bank he controlled in Temple. Then he forced the bank to loan him the money. In total, he took $156,000, plus the state lost a bunch of interest on the money. He's as crooked a politician as there is. Plus, he knows you won by a much larger total than his wife. He'll be trying to cause you trouble as soon as she gets into office."

"Well, Harris, I know a lot of people held their nose when they voted for her. But she was better than the Klan candidate, and most people are hoping that the Fergusons learned their lesson," said Dan.

"I wanted to give you the warning, Dan. We are all going to have to hope they learned their lesson. Because if they didn't, you are going to be right in the middle of the biggest controversy to hit Texas since the Ku Klux Klan."

11

Another Cloud on Texas

It was a beautiful spring day as the young attorney general walked up the tree-lined sidewalk to the state capitol. The magnificent pink granite structure resembled the only slightly larger United States Capitol in Washington, D.C. It stood more than 300 feet tall with a huge dome and two large three-story wings of offices. The Senate chambers were on the east side and the House chambers were on the west side. The governor's office and the attorney general's offices were on the first floor. Other state offices and the state supreme court and court of criminal appeals were located throughout the mammoth building.

Dan walked quickly to his offices. It had been three months since he had taken the oath of office as attorney general. He enjoyed his work and was eager to get started for the day.

"Good morning, General," called several of the state workers as they walked by. It was the custom to call the attorney general by the title of General, although Dan was uncomfortable with it and discouraged it whenever possible.

"Mr. May needs to visit with you this morning," Dan's secretary called out as Dan walked into his office.

"Okay, send him in," Dan replied.

Ernest May was an energetic assistant attorney general, one of three on Dan's staff, who worked long hours and was an aggressive lawyer.

"What's on your mind?" asked Dan.

"The governor," said Ernest.

"Not again. The people elected her, and it's not our job to undo the election. Remember, we aren't criminal prosecutors. We only do the state's legal business, contracts and such."

"But it's so frustrating to watch what's happening."

"The best I can tell, the Fergusons are behaving better than anyone should have expected. So far they have fired all the good state workers, hired their friends, and evened the score with The University of Texas by vetoing all money for the journalism, music, and library departments. Am I missing anything?" asked Dan with a grim smile.

"Yes, a whole lot. Jim is shaking down every contractor in the state to buy advertising in his newspaper, the *Ferguson Forum*. He's making every state employee pay for a subscription. He's fixing to rob the state blind on textbook purchases. He's taking $10,000 a year fees to do legal work for several railroads. Legal work? Can you imagine Jim Ferguson doing any work at all? And to top it all off, he is emptying the prison with pardons. They are outright selling those. Cash wrapped in newspaper goes into the governor's office and a pardon walks out."

"Well, that may be the capitol gossip, but none of that can be proved."

"Not yet."

"I am very concerned about those pardons. How many have there been?"

"It's up to 239 and climbing every day. The governor, Ma, that is, doesn't even do the orders. Jim writes it in pencil and then she takes a pen and writes over what he wrote. They don't even pretend she's governor."

"That's what the people voted for," Dan reminded Ernest. "It was better than the Klan."

"Not much."

"Well, we have plenty of state work to keep us busy. And I want you to get on with it. Remember, our boundary dispute with Oklahoma looks like it's working its way to the Supreme Court. We want to do our best on that one."

Ernest stood up to leave Dan's office. "I know we can't do anything about it, but it's frustrating working hard for the state while I know the Fergusons are stealing us blind."

"Which reminds me. You never mentioned the state highway commission. With all the road maintenance and new construction, their budget is around $20 million. If Jim Ferguson really wanted to steal a lot of money, that's where he'd have his best opportunity. You might want to keep your eyes on that part of state government."

Ernest smiled broadly. "Gotcha, boss."

It was four months later that Dan walked into Ernest May's office. It was the end of the work day, a long, hot, summer day in August. Ernest was talking with George Christian, one of the other assistant attorneys general.

"Ernest, George, you've worked enough today. We need to go take a walk," said Dan.

"You must be kidding," said Ernest. "It's too hot to walk. Besides, I still have a stack of work."

"It can wait. We are taking a walk," insisted Dan.

The three men left the capitol by the south entrance, past the governor's office, and took a short walk down Congress Avenue. They first passed the Travis County courthouse and then continued before they stopped in front of the Stephen F. Austin Hotel.

Dan looked at his two assistants. "Follow me, keep quiet, and don't look at or talk to anyone." The three men walked into the hotel lobby, got into the elevator, and rode up to the fourth floor. Dan led the men down the hall and took a key for room 432 out of his pocket. He looked both ways down the hall to make sure no one was watching. He unlocked the door, and the three of them entered.

"Gentlemen, I'd like you to meet Louis Kemp," Dan explained. "He's the executive director of the Texas Highway and Municipal Contractors Association."

Kemp was round and balding — round belly, round face, and a shiny, round head. He wore a bow tie.

As the men introduced themselves, there were three knocks on the door. Dan held up his hand, there was a pause, and then two more knocks. "That's a code we worked out," Dan said as he opened the door. A stenographer who worked for the state came in with her writing tablet.

"Let's all sit down, and Mr. Kemp can begin," said Dan.

Kemp looked at Dan as he spoke. "The state highway commission has three members. They control about $20 million worth of highway construction and maintenance contracts. All three members were appointed by Mrs. Ferguson. But the real power on the board is Jim Ferguson. He had himself named 'clerk,' and since then, all the commission meetings have been closed to the public. What few people have been allowed in the meetings say Jim does all the talking, makes all the decisions, and the commissioners sit there."

"That's not really illegal," said Ernest.

"Let me finish," said Kemp. "They immediately started awarding local maintenance contracts to companies no one has heard of. It's hard to figure out who owns them, but from what I can see, it's all friends of

136

Ferguson or people who buy a lot of advertising in his newspaper. Some of these contracts weren't even bid and in some, the contract was given to the highest bidder."

"How many contracts went to someone other than the lowest bidder?" asked Dan.

"Dozens," said Kemp. "The state is giving away thousands and thousands of dollars with those contracts."

"Well, I'm not district attorney anymore, but I can do something about state contracts. We'll be looking into that right away."

"But that's the tip of the iceberg," said Kemp. "The big money is on the resurfacing contracts. There are two companies, American Road and Hoffman Construction. They have contracts for millions, and they are overcharging."

"Mr. Kemp, cancelling a contract for not accepting the low bid is difficult legal work but it's even harder to prove overcharging — especially that the price is so high the contract should be cancelled. Somebody can always come up with an excuse why the price was so high."

"Mr. Moody," said Kemp. "Jim Ferguson is no dummy. But these contracts are outrageous. It's the same as stealing, and the state is going to lose millions."

"Okay, we have lots of work to do," said Dan. "Let's get down to details."

In mid-October, Dan, Ernest May, and George Christian met in Dan's capitol office. "We need to make our final decisions on how to proceed," Dan explained.

"Well, I'm done with the county maintenance contracts," said Ernest. "What I found was thirty-three counties where the contract was not given to

137

the low bidder. The price actually paid was $1,034,112, and the low bidders could have done it for $872,976.25. That means the state is overpaying by $161,135.75."

"Are the low bidders qualified?" asked Dan.

"Qualified and then some," said Ernest. "In most cases, they were awarded smaller contracts in other counties."

"Okay, I'll notify the highway commission tomorrow. Those contracts are illegal, and they need to be cancelled. George, how are we doing with American Road and Hoffman?"

"Exactly what Kemp told us we'd find. We are paying two or three times what that resurfacing work is worth," said George. "American Road is really an interesting company. It's got its corporation papers filed in Delaware, but its only business is with the Texas Highway Commission. The company didn't exist until the Fergusons got elected. They only own one piece of equipment, an asphalt machine."

"How do they do the work?" asked Dan.

"Oh, they contract it out to others. They rake in the profits. By the way, guess who they bought the asphalt machine from?"

"Frank Lanham," answered Ernest.

"Exactly," said George. "Frank Lanham, the chairman of the highway commission that gave them the contract."

"So how does Ferguson profit from all this?" asked Dan.

"Lots of ads in the *Ferguson Forum*, lots of jobs and contracts for his friends," said Ernest. "But my guess is there are some cash payments, probably very large payments, under the table. The kind we'll never be able to track down."

"Okay, let's let the local district attorney work on that," said Dan. "Tomorrow, I'll ask Lanham to stop payment on the thirty-three contracts, then let's get lawsuits ready to stop American Road and Hoffman. Maybe we can even get some of the money back. Some of those phony company executives might be getting pretty nervous."

Dan's office phone rang. His secretary informed him that George Christian was on the phone.

"George, how was your trip?"

"Couldn't have been better," replied George. "It went exactly like you planned."

"Tell me about it."

"I went right to their offices in Kansas City. Gave them your letter. Their faces turned white when they realized we had the whole swindle figured out. Then I gave them your offer. 'Give us all your cash and we'll put it in a joint account in Dallas until the lawsuit is over.' They asked me to leave the room. It was a very loud conversation. After about fifteen minutes, I was invited back in. They treated me real nice. I waited until someone returned from the bank."

"How much?"

"Try $436,000! Mostly cash, some securities."

"Wow!"

"You said 'wow' just thinking about it. You should see what it looks like when it's laid out on a table."

The Travis County courtroom was packed with reporters and spectators. Very unusual for a contract case. But this was no usual case.

Judge George Calhoun was on the bench. He looked out at the sea of spectators and the two tables full of lawyers in front of him.

"Let me review the facts," Judge Calhoun began. "Mr. Moody, you have filed this lawsuit as the state attorney general claiming that American Road Company made a huge, grossly unfair profit."

"Yes, your honor," replied Dan.

"Now, Mr. Worsham, you were hired by Mr. Lanham, at the direction of Governor Ferguson, and paid for by state money, to argue that the attorney general has no right to file this lawsuit."

"That's correct, your honor," replied the lawyer.

"And Mr. Carter, you're here representing the American Road Company," Judge Calhoun continued.

"Yes, sir," he responded.

"I have reviewed the law and heard your arguments. My ruling is that the attorney general is the only lawyer who is supposed to represent the state and therefore the governor's request is denied. Mr. Moody, you have the right to sue to cancel the contract and to recover damages, if you can prove your case."

Trial began two days later on November 19, 1925. Dan and Ernest called witnesses who testified that the Highway Commission, with its new members appointed by Governor Ma Ferguson and its new "clerk" Jim Ferguson, first met in February. They immediately closed the meeting to the public. Their first order of business was to award a contract to American Road to pave a thousand miles of state highway for thirty cents per square yard.

Dan called two road engineers to testify. The first was C. E. Hoff. Mr. Hoff explained that he was an experienced road engineer who had successfully completed many road projects.

"Have you examined the American Road contract?" asked Dan.

"Yes, I have."

"How long is the contract to last?"

"Two years."

"How much money would American Road be paid during that two years?"

"Approximately six million."

"Did you say six million?"

140

"Yes, sir. Six million dollars."

"What would a fair price, allowing for a good profit, be for that work?"

"Probably two million."

"They were overcharging the state about four million?"

"Only if the contract is completed."

"How did they figure the price?"

"I'm not sure. Resurface work can be done profitably for ten cents, maybe twelve cents a square yard. That's the figure every contractor in the state would be happy to do the work for."

The trial continued for several days, but the lawyers for American Road were never able to justify the price they charged. The case was being tried by Judge Calhoun without a jury. After the last witness testified, Judge Calhoun was ready to rule.

"Gentlemen, I'm ready to announce my ruling," Judge Calhoun began. "I don't see Mr. Moody in the courtroom. Does he want to be present, Mr. May?"

"I'm sure he wants to," said Ernest. "But his train left earlier this morning for Washington, D.C. He is going to argue the boundary dispute between Texas and Oklahoma in front of the United States Supreme Court."

"Very well," said the judge. Arguing in front of the United States Supreme Court was a high honor for any lawyer, and Judge Calhoun could well understand why Dan had left.

"After hearing the evidence, the court makes the following findings. The contract price paid in this case was grossly unfair and shocks the conscience of this court. The contract is hereby cancelled. The court further orders American Road to repay $650,000 to the State of Texas as damages. Finally, the court orders that the business charter of American Road to do business in Texas is cancelled. This company may never do business within the State of Texas again."

Ernest May and George Christian were eager to call their boss, but they waited two days until Dan finished his argument in front of the Supreme Court.

"Dan, it's good to hear your voice," said Ernest as he got him on the phone. George stood beside him, listening in.

"It's good to be talking to Austin," said Dan.

"How did the Supreme Court go?" asked Ernest.

"Fine. It was really a treat. The majesty of this building is something. I think they will rule in our favor. But tell me about political corruption in Texas."

"Judge Calhoun ruled in our favor."

"Yes, I read that in the papers. But that's the last news I got. What happened next?"

"Lanham and Burkett resigned the next morning. The papers are playing this up real big, and the average citizen is really tired of the Fergusons and their corrupt ways."

"How about Hoffman? Are we going to have to try them too?"

"I don't think so," said Ernest. "They asked to settle for several hundred thousand dollars plus cancellation of their business permit. Same as American Road."

"So, the final total will be what?" Dan asked.

"About a million cash returned to the state, cancellation of the contracts, two corrupt companies out of business, and two resignations from the highway commission."

"Sounds like the people finally won a round with the Fergusons," interjected Dan.

"Don't worry. There's plenty left to do. Remember the textbook contract you ruled illegal?"

"Sure. They were going to pay a nickel more than the store price for those spelling books. We should have gotten a huge discount on an order the size of the one the state placed."

"Well, Ma says you don't have any authority over it, and she ordered the contract paid." Before Dan could respond, Ernest rushed on. He and George had already talked this out. "Plus, they are selling pardons as fast as they can count the cash. They've already granted a thousand, and the number is still growing. Dan, if you want to stop the Fergusons from stealing the state blind, you better plan on running for governor."

12

A Return to Self-Respect

"Well, Dan, I hope you are ready 'cause the crowd is going wild!" announced Richard Critz.

Critz had entered the room in the Blazimar Hotel in downtown Taylor. Inside the room were Dan, along with his closest friends and advisors — the lawyers, Harry Graves and Richard Critz, part of the original Klan prosecution team, along with Harris Melasky and Lee Allen. Dan's new wife, Mildred Paxton, was on hand, as was his sister, Mary, and Mrs. Jesse Daniel Ames of Georgetown, one of the leaders in the fight for the rights of women to vote.

"Dan, I thought the crowd you had in Georgetown in March was great, but this crowd is fantastic. The train from San Antonio just arrived, and it looks like five hundred or more were on it," said Critz.

Dan went over to the window and looked out. It was indeed a massive crowd, and it was still growing. All of Main Street was blocked off, a huge platform had been built with red, white, and blue banners everywhere. A large star placed directly behind the podium said simply "Dan." Loudspeakers were set up throughout downtown.

"Harris, look out there," Dan said as he turned to look at his former law partner. "Remember when we were boys? We would be out there on market days, with hundreds of people and all the horses and wagons."

"Sure, we thought it was such a crowd then," said Harris. "Nothing compared to this crowd. There must be thousands in the street."

"I wonder if Mrs. Eckhardt is out there?" asked Critz as he walked toward the window, smiling at Dan.

"If she is, she's probably wishing she hadn't switched you so hard, Dan," said Harris.

"Oh, I doubt that. She enjoyed switching me. Besides, I *did* deserve it."

"It's time to go," said Critz. "We need to get up on the stage."

"Before we leave, Mrs. Ames, I want to thank you again for agreeing to make this speech tonight," said Dan.

"Oh, it's a pleasure, Mr. Moody. We worked very hard to get the right for women to vote. We know full well that the Fergusons were strongly opposed to us."

"Well, it's a big help to our campaign."

"Mr. Moody, I would truly like to see Texas have a woman governor. But Ma is a disgrace and their whole gang is a bunch of thieves stealing us blind. When we elect our next woman governor, it will be someone who will make us all proud."

Dan was awed by the size of the crowd as he took his seat on the platform. Richard Critz opened the rally with introductions. Mary and Mildred were both warmly applauded. Mrs. Ames made an eloquent speech but it was finally time for the main event. Dan was ready.

"Ladies and gentlemen, I present to you the finest attorney general our state has ever had, soon to be our finest governor, Taylor's own Dan Moody!"

The crowd went wild as Critz finished the introduction.

Dan's courtroom experience stood him well during the campaign. He was going to give a long speech, some two hours, but the crowd remained enthusiastic throughout.

"Two years ago, when I ran for attorney general, there was one issue in the campaign and one issue only. It was the Ku Klux Klan. Who was going to control the state, the people or some secret society of white bed-sheeted criminals? The people won. We took control of our government back and today, you would have trouble finding a dozen Klansmen still meeting!"

The crowd roared its approval.

"Now, as I run for governor, there is again one issue and one issue only. It's Fergusonism. Who is going to run the state? Should a paid employee of the railroad companies who is himself convicted and unable to hold office be running our state?"

"NO!"

"Do we want to pay millions of dollars extra to phony paving companies to maintain our roads?"

"NO!" the crowd roared.

"Do we want to cheat our children by wasting their education money on higher than retail-priced books from out of state companies?"

"NO!"

The following morning Dan met with his closest advisors at the Stephen F. Austin Hotel. Richard Critz, Harry Graves, Harris Melasky, and a few others were there.

"It couldn't have gone any better last night," said Harry.

"No, it couldn't have," said Dan. "But now it's

146

time to get to work. We have a campaign to run. Harris, what's the general assessment of the race?"

"It's an uphill race for you," said Harris. "Ferguson has a hardcore following among the rural farmers. They believe every word in the *Ferguson Forum,* and they believe nothing else. East Texas is tough for you. There is a lot of bootleg liquor in the Piney Woods and along the Louisiana border. They feel like they, or one of their kinfolk, might get caught, sent to prison and need to buy one of Ma's pardons. He's also got the state employees lined up. 'Course, he gave most of them their jobs. He's paid off the political bosses in South Texas, so you can imagine that Duval and Starr counties will be voting for him something like a thousand to two. He's working hard on the women vote, the Mexican vote, and he's always had the German vote."

"What about Lynch Davidson?" asked Dan.

"He's in the race to stay. He has unlimited personal money to spend, and you can bet he'll attack you the whole time. He thinks you are too young and he is the candidate to beat Ferguson."

"So, what does it all add up to?" asked Dan.

"A tough race," Harris replied.

"Don't you think that all the scandals will hurt him?" asked Richard Critz.

"Maybe in Austin," said Harris. "But no one was indicted, and people are already starting to forget them."

"Ferguson is also well organized," added Graves. "He's got a Ferguson man in every voting box in Texas to run his campaign."

"This is beginning to sound like our strategy sessions for the Klan trial," said Dan. "Remember, we weren't supposed to be able to convict the Klan."

All the men laughed.

"Okay, here's the strategy, gentlemen," began Dan. "Our friend Oscar Colquitt in Dallas is going to finance our own newspaper. He's calling it the *Free Lance*. It will be sent out to a couple of hundred thousand rural voters. It will lay out the truth about every nickel Jim Ferguson has stolen from the taxpayers. That will go after his main strength."

"I've talked to Mrs. Ames. She has Jane McCallum lined up. She's the most widely known, most respected woman in Texas political life. She's agreed to organize a Women for Moody drive," said Dan. "When Jane McCallum gets organized, even Jim Ferguson will watch out.

"Now, I want you to look through the *Ferguson Forum* and find all of Jim's disgusting, nasty editorials. I know he attacked the Jews once when he was mad about something, and I have one here where he attacks the Mexican people. He described them as 'blood thirsty' and generally attacked them as being uncivilized people. Take those editorials, don't add a single word or misquote him, and print them into pamphlets and circulate them among the people he was attacking. We'll see how many South Texas votes he gets when they see how he wrote that he would rather have, uh, here it is." Dan finished as he read from a *Ferguson Forum* clipping he had picked up. ". . . rather have 'a hundred Japs than a dozen Mexicans in Texas.'" Dan shook his head in disgust, then continued.

"Now, while you are doing that, I'll be in my Model-T, driving throughout the state. Get me five speeches a day. I'll make every one of them," said Dan.

"That's too hard of a pace," said Harry Graves.

"I'm young and I can do it," said Dan. "The newspapers are generally being supportive. I'll attack Fergusonism in every speech, and each day I'll add one more detail about the Ferguson corruption. The newspapers will give us a new headline every day.

148

Harris is right, people are already forgetting the scandals. But after a couple of months of daily headlines, people will hear 'Ferguson' and think 'thief,'" explained Dan. "Harris, I believe this strategy will attack every strength of Ferguson you mentioned."

"All except the South Texas bosses," said Harris.

"Well, we're not going to try to buy them off. I'd rather lose than pay tribute to Archie Parr. Those are bought votes and we will let Ferguson have them," said Dan. "One last thing. That campaign slogan, 'Dan's the Man.' It's catchy and it looks good in those bright red letters on the white background. Let's get the sticker out all over Texas. Get it painted on buildings and barns where you can. I don't want a Texan to be able to drive a quarter mile without seeing that slogan."

Dan took to the road. He made five speeches a day. In between, he stopped in towns to shake hands. Every speech, he attacked Fergusonism.

"There is one issue and one issue only. It is Fergusonism," he continually said. And each day, he added new details of the scandals to his speech — an overpriced textbook, a state contractor forced to buy an ad in the *Ferguson Forum*, a payoff to get a state job, a sold pardon — Dan kept the heat on. The newspapers printed his attacks each day. As May ended, the crowds were growing bigger and bigger.

Governor Ma Ferguson did not make political speeches. She left that up to Jim. When she did speak, it was merely to introduce her husband.

On May 22, Mrs. Ferguson did make a short speech before a huge crowd in the small town of Sulphur Springs, which was a hotbed of Ferguson supporters. It was to be the opening of her campaign. She issued a challenge.

149

"If I lose the July 24th primary by even a single vote, I will pledge to resign my office immediately and not stay on until my term ends in January. Provided, that is, I lead him by twenty-five thousand votes, he will resign immediately."

Dan immediately accepted the challenge in his next speech. "I will be justifiably criticized by some because the governorship is not to be wagered. But if it means bringing Fergusonism to an end six months early, it is worth it."

The campaign continued. Mrs. Ferguson did not campaign but Jim set up forty-three speaking engagements, beginning June 2 in Beaumont and ending July 23 in Austin.

Jim's attacks were bombastic and personal. At every speech he called Dan a boy.

"He has nothing to recommend him save a lipstick, a new wife, and a big head," said Ferguson. He attacked Mildred, claiming she would henpeck Dan and be chasing him around the governor's mansion with a rolling pin.

It was mid-July, two weeks before the primary, when Dan was in Austin and met again with his advisors in the Stephen F. Austin Hotel. Critz, Melasky, Graves, and Mrs. McCallum were there when Dan arrived.

Dan was wearing his white linen suit, a crisp, clean shirt, and a straw hat. "You look as cool and confident as anyone has ever been during a Texas summer," Richard Critz said.

"I am enjoying every minute of this campaign. The people have finally figured out what a crook Ferguson is," said Dan.

"That's the reports we are getting from everywhere," said Harris Melasky. "Your message is getting out all over the state and people are flocking to you."

"Mr. Moody, you can't imagine how the women of Texas are responding," said Mrs. McCallum. "We had 200 ladies at a Moody meeting at the Driskill Hotel, and we have a rally set for Eastwood Park the week before the election."

"Wonderful, Mrs. McCallum," said Dan. "I can't thank you enough for your help."

"All of your strategy is paying off," said Harris. "East Texas, some German votes, and maybe the Archie Parr votes in South Texas are Ferguson's only strengths."

"Oh yes," said Harry Graves. "Your 'Dan's the Man' stickers are everywhere."

"All except East Texas," added Harris. "They have 'Me for Ma' stickers up there." They all laughed.

"Well, I'm going to keep up my schedule," said Dan. "I think Fergusonism is dead. But the real question is, are we going to win without a run-off?"

"Yes, and Ferguson knows it. He's really turning his speeches into a circus act," said Harris. "He was in Lufkin last week with two monkeys on the stage. He accused you of being in league with 'monkey-faced Baptists' and the Ku Klux Klan. He accused you right out of being a Klansman or at least a sympathizer."

"I don't suppose anyone has a stronger anti-Klan reputation than you do, Dan," said Harry Graves.

"Yes, well, they are desperate. But none of their personal attacks are going to stick," said Dan. "We are going to end Fergusonism and bring honesty back to the governor's mansion."

Dan continued his near frenzied campaign schedule. He finished the last weeks up with a final trip around the state — speeches in Denison, Fort Worth, and Dallas before returning to Austin to begin the last day of the campaign.

On Friday morning, Mildred, Mary, and Dan all went out onto a balcony at the Stephen F. Austin Hotel. They looked out over the two thousand who gathered for one of Dan's final speeches. Mildred and Mary both thanked the crowd. Dan added his thank you, predicted a great victory, and pledged to return honesty and decency to the Governor's office. Dan then sped off on another two hundred-mile trip to make speeches in two more county seats, La Grange and Lockhart. Even on the last day of the campaign, Dan would not rest. On election day, after Dan and Mildred voted in Taylor, they went to the Blazimar Hotel to meet with a group of supporters.

There was a front page editorial in the *Austin-American Statesman* Sunday edition that told the story of the election. It was headlined: "A Great Victory." The editorial continued:

> The voters of the state Saturday met the issue of Fergusonism in direct and overwhelming fashion. They registered in emphatic manner their lack of confidence in the unofficial and irresponsible administration of James E. Ferguson by a vote of more than two to one . . . Dan Moody is to be congratulated for the courageous battle . . . He is to be congratulated on being the youngest man ever called to the governor's chair . . . But the men and women who supported his cause are still more to be congratulated . . . in passing over the minor issue of youth and inexperience in meeting the major issue of direct and clean government.

The *El Paso Times and Herald* comment about Dan's victory was even more direct. "Texas has recovered her self-respect."

It would be two weeks before the final election results were in. Dan had won 409,732 votes to Mrs. Ferguson's 283,482. But the other four candidates had enough votes to keep Dan 1,771 votes short of fifty percent. In fact, it was only the Fergusons' dishonesty that had kept Moody from winning without a run-off. The Fergusons had paid off the political bosses in Duval and Starr counties, where Mrs. Ferguson won by a combined 2,163 to 41. That 2,122-vote margin was all that kept Dan from winning without a run-off. But the final election results required a run-off — unless Mrs. Ferguson honored her wager to resign immediately if she lost the primary by even one vote.

"Well, Dan, you can relax now," Harris told Dan. "She surely will not subject herself to another defeat in the run-off."

"Don't be sure. The Fergusons aren't used to doing honorable or decent things."

"You are the toast of the country. Newspapers around the country are hailing your victory. 'Young, aggressive attorney general beats corruption.' There is even mention of you as a presidential candidate for 1928."

"Well, Harris, I'm not going to get all caught up in it. I did enjoy being asked to throw out the first pitch at the Austin Senators game the other night."

A few days later, Mrs. Ferguson announced that the race had been stolen from her by the Ku Klux Klan, and she would remain in it. Dan resumed his non-stop campaign while Jim Ferguson made only a few speeches. When the votes were counted, the Moody landslide buried Mrs. Ferguson 495,723 to 270,595. Fergusonism was defeated.

"He did *what*?!" Dan's scream could be heard outside the attorney general's capitol office. Ernest May had just broken the bad news to him.

"He pardoned Murray Jackson," Ernest repeated.

Dan was furious. "Even for Jim Ferguson that's a

new low. Pardoning a Klansman. With the appeals and all, he's barely served a year in prison!"

"It's worse, Dan. His, rather her, official statement says the pardon was because there was substantial evidence that he was innocent."

"Innocent!" screamed Dan. "There never was a more guilty man than Murray Jackson. Our trial evidence was overwhelming."

Ernest had never seen Dan so worked up. All through the campaign, even when Ferguson was taunting him about his new wife, Dan had kept his cool.

By this time, George Christian had entered the room. "The press is on the phone. They want your reaction to the Jackson pardon," said George.

"Everyone, please leave," asked Dan. "I need to be alone. Tell the press we'll call them back later."

Dan spent most of the next hour alone in his office. He then summoned Ernest and George.

"I've thought this over. When I set out to prosecute the Klan, they had 170,000 Texas members. They controlled local elections, and Klan violence was a way of life. Only three years later, you can't find a Klansman. We won. As for justice, the four we convicted each served at least a year in prison. That's probably as much justice as we can expect with a Ferguson as governor.

"Call the press and tell them our only comment is that the Fergusons are still governor for two more months. We will all have to wait and see what they do."

* * * * *

It was a crisp January morning in 1931. Austin was still asleep as the Moody family woke up and began their last morning in the governor's mansion. The huge antebellum home, with its white columns, spacious grounds, and gracious shade trees com-

154

manded a beautiful view of Austin from its location on the high ground across the street from the southwest corner of the capitol.

"Is this what you expected when we got married?" Dan asked Mildred as they stood together on the second-floor balcony, looking down towards Congress Avenue.

Mildred laughed. "I didn't know what to expect after that whirlwind campaign."

"We will always have a lot of pleasant memories of this house. It will be where we lived when Dan, Jr. was born, and we spent our first four years of married life."

"Yes, and I was the gracious first lady of Texas, queen of the State." Mildred laughed again. "If people only knew what it was like changing diapers, making homemade sandwiches, and entertaining the state's leaders with no money."

"Thankfully, Mary and the Austin and Taylor ladies were always there to pitch in with the food."

"They knew we could barely feed and clothe our family on the $4,000 salary the governor makes. I certainly can see how the Fergusons could have spent some of the money they stole just on hiring caterers for their parties."

"The Driskill lost a good customer when the Fergusons moved out," said Dan with a smile.

"But some of my fondest memories of this house will be working with the ladies in our cramped kitchen, getting the last of the sandwiches on trays, and trying to keep my gown from getting food on it."

"Mildred, I know you have a lot still to do this morning. I've got to leave now and meet with Harris and Richard one last time in the Sam Houston room."

"We will have to toast the governor with our coffee cups," said Harris Melasky as he and Richard Critz

155

rose, cups in hand, when Dan walked into the room. Sam Houston, the hero of the Texas Revolution, was one of Texas' first governors. The room was an elegant sitting room with a huge portrait of Houston on one wall.

"Enough of that," said Dan. "Let's sit down and enjoy our last morning. Ross will make a fine governor, but I'm sure with all his millions he won't enjoy the mansion nearly as much as we have."

The men sat down. "Richard, appointing you judge of the appeals court was the best appointment I've made as governor, and Harris, you seem to have the Midas touch the way your law practice and business interests have made you a wealthy man. As for me, I'm flat broke. I have a wife and child to support, and I sure hope I have a paying client in my new law office tomorrow."

"Oh, poor Dan Moody," kidded Harris. "The newspapers say you were one of our most successful and popular governors ever. You were re-elected with a huge majority two years ago, and you could have been the first to win a third term if you had run again."

"Yes, a third term, and I would have been broker still," said Dan. "Two terms is enough. I'll just be Dan Moody, lawyer, from now on."

"And you will be one of the most successful lawyers the state has ever had too," said Richard. "You will have plenty of paying clients."

"You have both been with me the whole time, from our storage room law office, the Klan trials, and all the political campaigns. It's been an amazing ten years."

"And well worth it," added Harris.

"Gentlemen, I hate to break this up, but the governor needs to dress for Ross' inauguration," said Mildred as she came to the doorway.

A few minutes later, Dan was by himself upstairs as he finished dressing. He walked out onto the balcony and looked over towards the capitol. The newspapers could list his accomplishments as reorganizing the highway department, raising teachers' salaries, and improving education. But Dan knew that his biggest accomplishment had been to rid the state of the Fergusons and restore honesty to the governor's office. It hadn't been easy. Mildred and Mary and all those volunteers from Taylor had entertained thousands, all with donated food. New clothes were a rarity and luxuries unheard of for the Moodys. But Dan had been honest to the penny.

Dan went into the bedroom for his final official act as governor. He marked a passage in the Neff Bible. It was a tradition that Governor Pat Neff had begun that each outgoing governor mark a passage for the new governor. Dan underlined the sixteenth verse of the third chapter of the book of John. It was a verse he used frequently in his Sunday school class.

He returned to the balcony and looked at the capitol one final time. He thought again of all he had been through during his lifetime. All the times he had been told that he was too young or that something was impossible. Too young for law school, too young for county attorney, too young for attorney general, too young for governor. Impossible to convict the Klan, impossible to end corruption in government.

He had proved everyone wrong. He had defeated the Klan; he had defeated the Fergusons. He had given Texas back her self-respect.

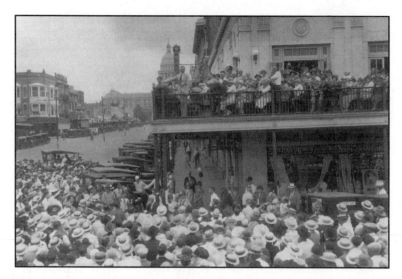

Moody, standing on the balcony of the Stephen F. Austin Hotel, addresses a crowd of supporters on Congress Avenue during the 1926 race for governor. Photo courtesy of Austin History Center, Austin Public Library.

Market days in downtown Taylor in 1923. The cars and dress were typical of the 1920s period described in this story. Photo courtesy of Taylor Public Library, Archives Section.

Where Were the Women?

Can you imagine a "men's only" club? The courts sure seemed that way back in the 1920s. All of the participants in the Murray Jackson trial — the judge, seven prosecutors, six defense attorneys, and twelve jurors — were all men. What a contrast to today, when women play such a vital role in our legal system!

Hortense Ward of Houston, who was licensed in 1910, is usually credited with being the first woman lawyer in Texas. She had a long and active legal career. By 1923, there may have been thirty women lawyers in Texas. None of them were judges. Women could vote in all elections by 1920, but were not allowed to serve on juries until 1954.

The first full-time female judge was Sarah T. Hughes of Dallas, who served as a district court judge from 1934 to 1946. As a federal judge, she is best known for administering the presidential oath to Vice-President Lyndon B. Johnson in 1963.

Today, there are over 15,000 female lawyers in Texas. Two women, Sandra Day O'Connor and Ruth Bader Ginsberg, serve on the U.S. Supreme Court. Both of Texas' two highest courts have women judges. Rose Spector, Priscilla Owen, and Deborah Hankinson serve on the Texas Supreme Court, and Sharon Keller and Sue Holland serve as judges on the Texas Court of Criminal Appeals. Harriet Miers and Colleen McHugh have served as presidents of the State Bar of Texas, and Becky McPherson was the 1997 president of the Texas District and County Attorneys Association.

Being a lawyer can be an exciting, rewarding career, in which you can right wrongs, correct unfairness, and seek justice. And the opportunities are unlimited, whether you're a boy or a girl!

This march by hooded Klansmen down Austin's Congress Avenue was typical of Klan parades held throughout the United States during the early 1920s. Photo courtesy of Austin History Center, Austin Public Library.

Dan Moody taking the oath of office as Texas governor. Moody was the first governor to be sworn in at an outdoor ceremony. Photo courtesy of Austin History Center, Austin Public Library.

Glossary

alien: a Klan term which referred to any non-Klan member.

bootlegger: someone who makes or sells alcoholic beverages. Manufacture and sale of alcohol was illegal in the United States during the 1920s.

carpetbagger: a Northerner who came to the South after the Civil War for the purpose of making a financial profit by taking advantage of the problems caused by the war.

charge of the court: written directions from the judge explaining to the jury what the law is and telling the jury what questions they should answer.

citizen: a Klan term which referred to a Klan member.

contempt: an order from a judge which punishes someone for refusing to obey a judge's order. Usually, the judge orders someone held in jail until they obey the order.

county attorney: an elected county official who prosecutes misdemeanor crimes.

cross-examination: questioning of the witness by either the prosecutor or the defense attorney, whoever did not call the witness to testify.

district attorney: an elected official who often represents more than one county, who prosecutes felony crimes.

dry goods store: a store that sells clothing and small

personal items that are not sold at a food or hardware store.

Exalted Cyclops: president of a local Klan chapter.

felony: a more serious criminal offense. The crimes carry punishments that include long sentences in state prison.

flogging: whipping with some type of strap.

grand jury: a group of twelve citizens who must determine if there is enough evidence to bring felony criminal charges against a person.

immunity: an order from a judge that prevents someone from being tried for a crime based on information the judge orders the defendant to provide.

indictment: a piece of paper that contains the legal charges against a criminal defendant. An indictment can only be issued by a grand jury. It is required for felony charges.

Klabee: treasurer of a local Klan chapter.

Klaliff: vice-president of a local Klan chapter.

Klankraft: all practices and ideas of the Klan.

Klavern: local meeting place for Klan chapter.

Kleagle: a Klan recruiter.

Klectoken: the $10 Klan initiation fee.

Kligrapp: secretary of the local Klan chapter.

Klokann: the executive committee of a local Klan chapter. It was made up of the Exalted Cyclops and all the other officers of the chapter.

Klonversation: exchange of greetings by use of acronyms. For example, AYAK meant "Are you a Klansman?"

Kloran: the ritual book of the Klan.

Kloxology: a religious song used at the end of a Klan meeting.

Kludd: chaplain of the local Klan chapter.

Konklave: any Klan chapter meeting.

Liberty League: a group that opposed the Ku Klux Klan.

misdemeanor: a less serious type of criminal offense. These crimes carry punishments of a fine only or a local jail sentence of a year or less.

perjury: lying by a witness who has taken an oath to tell the truth.

primary election: an election where members of a political party choose a person to run for a political office.

rebuttal: evidence offered by either the prosecutor or the defense attorney to explain or contradict evidence offered by the other side.

recess: a break in the trial ordered by the judge.

run-off election: a second primary election which is held between the top two vote getters only if no candidate receives more than fifty percent of the votes in a primary election.

scalawag: a white Southerner who took advantage of the problems caused by the Civil War for his own personal gain.

verdict: the decision of a jury.

vigilante: a person who takes the law into his own hands by seeking to punish criminals without following any laws or court procedures.

Bibliography

Books:

Alexander, Charles. *The Ku Klux Klan in the Southwest.* Norman: University of Oklahoma Press, 1996.

Brown, Norman. *Hood, Bonnet and Little Brown Jug.* College Station: Texas A&M Press, 1984.

Humphrey, David C. *Austin: An Illustrated History.* Northridge: Windsor Publications, 1985.

McKay, Seth. *Texas Politics.* Lubbock: Texas Tech Press, 1952.

Mantor, Ruth. *Our Town: Taylor.* Taylor, 1983.

Paulissen, May Nelson and Carl McQueary. *Miriam.* Austin: Eakin Press, 1995.

Rutherford, Bruce. *The Impeachment of Jim Ferguson.* Austin: Eakin Press, 1983.

Scarbrough, Clara Stearns. *Land of Good Water Takahue Pousetsu.* Georgetown, Texas: SunPublishing, 1973.

Tyler, Ron, ed. *The New Handbook of Texas.* Austin: The Texas State Historical Association, 1996.

Welch, June Rayfield. *The Texas Governors.* Dallas: GLA Press, 1977.

Newspapers:

Austin American (various dates 1921-31)
Austin Statesman (various dates 1921-31)
Taylor Daily Press (various dates 1920-27)
Williamson County Sun (various dates 1920-27)

Other Sources:

Moody file, Austin History Center, Austin Public Library, Austin, Texas.

Moody file, Center for American History, The University of Texas at Austin.

Moody files and exhibits, Moody Museum, Taylor, Texas.

State v. Murray Jackson, trial transcript, Texas State Archives, Austin, Texas.

State v. A. A. Davis, trial transcript, Texas State Archives, Austin, Texas.

State v. Murray Jackson, No. 9449; *State v. Olen Gossett*, No. 9450; *State v. Dewey Ball*, No. 9451; *State v. A. A. Davis*, No. 9520, District Clerk Files, Georgetown, Texas.

Places to Visit

Governor Dan Moody Birthplace Museum, 114 West 9th Street, Taylor, TX 76574 (512) 352-8654; for tour arrangements call (512) 856-0123. The museum is open for special events and tours.

Williamson County Courthouse, 706 Main Street, Georgetown, TX 78626. The courtroom where Moody prosecuted the Klan is located on the second floor; it is currently used as a justice of the peace courtroom.

Texas State Capitol, 11th Street and Congress Avenue, Austin, TX 78701 (512) 463-0063. Free guided tours of the building are available 8:30 A.M. to 4:30 P.M. Monday through Friday and on weekends from 9:30 A.M. to 4:30 P.M.

Governor's Mansion, 11th and Lavaca Street, Austin, TX 78701 (512) 463-5518. Open for tours Monday through Friday, 10:00 A.M. to 11:40 A.M. Closed on state holidays and for official functions.

Texas State Cemetery, 7th and Comal, Austin, TX (512) 478-0098. Governor Moody and his wife Mildred are buried on a hillside about thirty feet south of the Stephen F. Austin statue and grave. The cemetery also has a visitors center with exhibits. Open Monday through Saturday, 8:00 A.M. to 5:00 P.M., Sundays and holidays, 9:00 A.M. to 6:00 P.M.

About the Author

Ken Anderson holds the same district attorney's job that Dan Moody had seventy-five years ago. As a young assistant district attorney with a quiet voice, Ken was frequently told by Judge William S. Lott, "Speak up! When Dan Moody was district attorney, you could hear him across the street."

Like a lot of dads with two boys, Ken coaches basketball and baseball. He has spoken at over 200 fifth-grade DARE graduations; he sponsors a middle school anti-drug poster contest; and he frequently goes to high schools to talk about driving and alcohol. He does a mock trial involving a fifth-grade class called "The Stolen Peanut Butter and Jelly Sandwich Caper." Ken is also very active as a Sunday School teacher in his church. He has started up a children's advocacy center for juvenile crime victims. Also, Ken went online with a special kids' web site: www.wilco.org/kids.

Ken wrote this book for kids because a lot of the things he talks about at schools — sticking up for what's right and staying with your goals no matter what — are things that Dan Moody had to deal with. He also wrote it because when Ken was a kid, the words he most hated were, "You can't do that!" Dan Moody was told he was too young and couldn't achieve, but he showed everyone that he could.